SOUTH CAROLINA GUN LAW
First Edition

© Copyright 2009 by: Stephen Fulton Shaw,
James Patrick Kelley, &
G. Curtis Moore, Jr.

Important Information on Updates

The authors and Legislative Consultant have thoroughly researched the information in this book. However, statutes can be amended and new case law created. While the law generally moves slowly, changes do happen and they can happen abruptly. Please look for annual updates of this book at your local gun shop, online, or at gun shows. The authors also recommend that you visit the GrassRoots GunRights of South Carolina website (**SCFirearms.org**) frequently to keep abreast of current topics regarding South Carolina gun legislation and court activity. Although the authors recommend the above website as a reference, the authors, Legislative Consultant Robert D. Butler, D.C., J.D., and GrassRoots GunRights of South Carolina are completely separate entities and you should assume no express or implied relationship between them. Further, the authors and Legislative Consultant make no express or implied warranty as to the accuracy or completeness of the website's information.

FOR MORE INFORMATION ABOUT THIS BOOK VISIT:

SCGunLaw.com

SHAW & KELLEY PUBLISHING

P.O. Box 744
Mauldin, SC 29662

ISBN 978 – 0 – 9817469 – 0 – 6

Warnings & Disclaimer:

The authors and Legislative Consultant have thoroughly and extensively researched the materials in this book to ensure accuracy. However, the authors, Legislative Consultant, publisher, distributors, references, links and retailers specifically disclaim and assume no liability or responsibility whatsoever for its use, reliance on its contents, reliance on any subsequent editions or updates nor do they assume any liability or responsibility for errors, inaccuracies, omissions, misrepresentations or any inconsistency contained herein. Further, the authors, Legislative Consultant, publisher, distributors, references, links and retailers specifically disclaim any and all possible liability premised upon reliance of this book, or any updates, including, but not limited to, liability for negligence or gross negligence. This book, along with any subsequent updates, is not rendered as legal advice, it is general information developed by the authors, and should not be relied upon as legal advice. For legal advice, an attorney should always be consulted regarding specific questions and how your specific questions relate to specific facts, instances and circumstances. This is especially true because the law changes and some legal advice can only be given when an attorney knows the subtleties of your particular question. Moreover, legal opinions sometimes vary and the opinion of one attorney might differ from another attorney's opinion. Any and all warranties, express or implied, including those for implied warranty of fitness for a particular purpose and implied warranty of merchantability are expressly herein disclaimed.

This book is copyrighted work protected under the laws of the United States of America, and no part of the book may be reproduced in print, photocopy, electronically, on the internet or otherwise without first obtaining the express written permission of the authors.

ISBN 978-0-9817469-0-6 $19.95

Dedication

This book is dedicated to Melanie Donna Moore: cherished wife, sister and friend of the authors.

Table of Contents

Important Information on Updates i
Warnings & Disclaimer: ii
Dedication iii
Forward xi
Chapter 1 1
  The Right to Keep and Bear Arms 1
    The Natural Right to Personal Defense 1
    American Character 1
    Articles of Confederation 2
    United States Constitution 2
      Anti-Individual Gun Rights Obfuscation 2
    Historical Context of the Second Amendment 3
      Additional Support of the Right 4
    Current Activity of the United States Supreme Court 5
    The South Carolina Constitution 7
      The Police Power of the States 7
    The South Carolina Code of Laws 8
    County and Municipal Home Rule Power 8
    State Law Trumps Local Ordinances 9
    Confiscation of Firearms 9
    Conclusion 10
Chapter 2 11
  Legal Requirements for Buying a Gun and Ammunition 11
    Gun Sellers 11
      Age for Purchasing from a Federally Licensed Dealer 12
    Age Requirement for Purchase from Private Individual 13
    Residency 14
    Must be a Resident or Military to Buy a Pistol from a Dealer 15
    Dealers Cannot Deal in Handguns Made from Certain Metals 16
    Inheritance 17
    NFA Machine Gun Trust 17
    Registration of Guns 18
    Conclusion 18
Chapter 3 20
  Legal Disabilities and Executive Clemency 20
    What is a Legal Disability? 20
    What is the Lifetime Federal Firearms Disability? 20
    The Legal Danger of Domestic Violence 23
    How Do I Remove a Legal Disability? 24

Chapter 4..25
  Concealed Weapons Permit..25
    Introduction 25
    What Does the Permit Allow? 26
    What does Concealable Weapon Mean?...26
    What does Concealed Mean? 27
    What Does the Permit NOT Allow? 28
    Qualifications 28
    The Application Process 29
    The Application Form 30
    Arrests, Pleas, Convictions and Traffic Tickets 31
    Residency and Proof of Residency 32
    Resident...33
    Military Resident 33
    Non-US Citizens...34
    Qualified Non-Resident..34
    Getting Qualified Non-Resident Paperwork from Government Offices 35
    Photographs...36
    Proof of Adequate Vision 37
    Proof of Firearms Training..37
    Basic Training Provided by CWP Class 37
    Alternative Proof of Training 40
    Fingerprints 41
      Exception to the Fingerprint Requirement..42
    Application Fee..43
    The Role of SLED in Approval or Denial...43
    Once You Get Your Permit...45
    What if I am Approached by a Law Enforcement Officer? 46
    The CWP Statute vs. Carrying Under an Exception 46
    Carrying Under the CWP Statute...47
    Carrying Under a Statutory Exception...47
    What if I have a Concealed Weapon when my Buddy is Pulled Over? 48
    The Practical Elements of a Law Enforcement Officer Road Stop 49
    CWP vs. Exception Flow-Chart..50
    Carrying without having the CWP Card with You..52
    What if an Officer Wants Me to Get Out of the Car to Check Me for Weapons?
   52
    What if a Police Officer wants to Search my Car? 53
    Law Enforcement Officers can be Wrong...55
    Unlawful Places to Carry Even with a Concealed Weapons Permit..............55
    Special Permission 58

Special Privileges for Some Permit Holders 59
Can I Carry into a U.S. Post Office? 60
Retail Mail Stores 61
Carrying at a Bank or ATM Machine.. 61
Credit Unions 62
Businesses that Serve Alcohol on the Premises...................................... 62
Businesses that Do Not Want You to Carry in Their Building 64
   Required Sign 66
Penalty for Carrying into a Prohibited Business 67
Lawsuit Protection for Business Owners... 67
Business Owners, Managers and Employees 69
   Guns at Work Chart 71
Other People's Homes or Dwellings 72
From Car to Home and Vice Versa with a Permit.................................. 72
Partial Exception for CWP Holders on the Capitol Grounds.................. 72
Permit Reciprocity with Other States 73
Carrying in North Carolina and Georgia... 74
Renewal of the South Carolina Concealed Weapons Permit.................... 75
Lost or Stolen Permit.. 76
Permit Holder List is not Public Information 77
Chapter 5.. 79
Possessing and Transporting Guns without a Permit............................. 79
Handguns 79
Handguns in Your Home 80
Handguns and Firearms in Foster Homes 81
Handguns in Other People's Homes with Permission............................. 82
Group Child Care Homes... 82
Child Care Centers 82
Business Owners Bringing Handguns to Work 83
Defining Fixed Place of Business... 85
Employees Bringing Handguns to Work... 86
Handguns at Businesses that Serve Alcohol.. 87
Who can carry a handgun onto the premises of a business that serves alcohol? ...88
Automobiles and Other Private Conveyances... 89
Vehicle Trunks vs. SUV Luggage Compartments 89
Guns on the Seat, Floor or Door Pocket of a Car 91
Traveling Out of South Carolina 91
   Does the Federal Law Protect You? 92
   Carrying Pursuant to a CWP and Reciprocity................................. 92
   Interstate Travel Scenarios under the FOPA 93
   Defining Destination States 96

Rules for Transporting Interstate under the FOPA 97
Motorcycles 98
Private Boats 98
Aircraft and Airports 99
Public Transportation.. 103
The Rules for Schools... 104
Criminal Penalties for Guns on School Grounds............................. 104
    Off Campus Events 105
    Driving Through a Campus 106
    Exception for Permission from Authorities in Charge of the Premises.......... 107
    Exception for Law Enforcement and Guards 108
    Exception for Military and Military Science.............................. 109
    Exception for Married Students 109
    No Deadly Weapons on Elementary and Secondary School Grounds.......... 110
    Expulsion for Bringing a Firearm to a Public School 111
    Deadly Weapons, other than Firearms, at College 112
Can I Carry on the Capitol Grounds in Columbia?......................... 112
Hotels, Motels and Lodging 113
National Parks, Forests and Wildlife Refuges 114
Hunting in National Forests.. 115
State Forests and State Parks (There is a Difference!) 116
State Farmer's Markets 117
Pepper Spray 118
Statutory Carry Exceptions.. 119
Law Enforcement Officer as a Party to a Civil or Criminal Action 123
Mailing Guns... 123
Minimum Age for Possession of Guns.. 124
Train Children about Guns 127
Conclusion 127
Chapter 6... 128
Weapon Crimes and Lawsuits... 128
Criminal Law versus Civil Liability 128
Reminder about the Lifetime Federal Firearms Disability............... 130
Pointing a Gun at Someone 130
Entering the Residence of Others while Armed 131
Criminal Negligence.. 131
Discharging a Gun into a Dwelling, Building or Vehicle 132
Taking a Law Enforcement Officer's Weapon 132
Guns at School 135
Public Buildings... 137
No Firearms on the Capitol Grounds 137

Trap Guns.. 137
Forfeiture of Weapon if Crime involves Concealed Weapons 138
Additional Penalty for Firearms in Business that Sell Alcohol 139
Drinking and Shooting.. 139
Possessing a Firearm while Unlawfully Dealing in Alcohol 141
Discharging a Firearm within 50 yards of a Public Road while Drunk 141
Allowing Mental Patients and Mental Prisoners Access to Firearms 142
Providing Prisoners with Firearms... 143
Criminally Negligent use of a Firearm before, during or after Hunting............. 144
Discharging a Firearm at a Boat Ramp or Landing.. 145
Teaching, Demonstrating, or Making a Firearm for Civil Disorder 146
Increased Penalty for using Concealed Weapon in Violent Crimes.................. 147
Tear Gas and Chemical Irritant Weapons 148
Objects Designed to Cause Damage by Fire or Detonation 149
Transfer of Handguns to Convicts, Minors & Mentally Incompetents............. 150
What if I Find a Gun? 151
Machine Guns, Military and Sawed-Off Weapons.. 152
    Acquiring Machine Guns or NFA Restricted Guns through Inheritance...... 153
Barrel Length under the NFA 153
Military-Type Accessories under the NFA 154
Possession of a Firearm by those Convicted of Certain Crimes 154
Armor Piercing Bullets 155
Illegal to Provide Guns to Illegal Aliens... 156
Possessing Stolen Handguns.. 157
Possessing Handguns with Altered Serial Numbers....................................... 157
Shooting at Trains 157
Legal Defense to a Crime 158
Civil Lawsuit Liability... 158
A Note about Keeping Guns Away from Children.. 160
Will my Insurance Cover Me if I get Sued or Arrested? 161
Chapter 7.. 164
  Self-Defense 164
    Introduction 164
    The Unfortunate Context of Self-Defense 165
    Distinction between Deadly and Non-Deadly Force............................ 167
    The Four Elements of Self-Defense in South Carolina............................ 168
      Without Fault.. 169
      Belief of Imminent Threat of Death or Serious Bodily Harm 170
        Imminent Threat Presumed in Home, Dwelling or Occupied Vehicle... 172
      The "Reasonable" or "Prudent Man" Standard.............................. 174
        Reasonable Fear Presumed in Home, Dwelling or Occupied Vehicle 175

Legal Presumptions.. 176
   No Other Probable Means of Avoiding the Danger 177
More on the Protection of Persons and Property Act....................... 180
Self-Defense against Non-Deadly Attacks 184
The "Alter-Ego" Rule.. 185
The Danger of Defending Others under the Alter-Ego Rule............. 185
Preventing the Commission of a Violent Crime................................. 186
Protecting Yourself or Others versus Protecting Property................. 186
Criminal and Civil Liability 188
Complete Defense to Criminal and Civil Action 188
Excusable Homicide 189
Criminal Manslaughter 189
Civil Negligence.. 190
Display of Weapons.. 190
What if I Shoot Someone in Self-Defense? 191
Why You Must Never Talk with the Police or Anyone Else 191
Homeowner's, Auto, and Umbrella Insurance Policies...................... 201
Simple Rules for Making Sense of Self-Defense 201
Conclusion 202
Chapter 8.. 204
  Miscellaneous Gun Related Laws.. 204
The Shooting Range Protection Act of 2000 204
Civil Lawsuit Protection for Gun and Ammunition Manufacturers ... 206
Local Governments cannot Confiscate Guns during an Emergency... 206
Assault Weapons Ban... 207
Making Modifications to Semi-Automatic Assault Rifles................... 208
The Law Enforcement Officers Safety Act 209
Proposed National Right to Carry Law 212
Security Officers and Private Security Companies 213
   Security Weapons Permit 214
   Security *Concealed* Weapons Permit 217
Chapter 9.. 219
  Conclusion 219
Your Brain is your First Line of Defense.. 219
What You should have Learned from this Book 219
The Bottom Line 220
Appendix I 221
  Federal Firearms Disability and Removing a Legal Disability............. 221
Federal Firearms Disability in General... 221
How do you know if you have a legal disability? 222
What is a crime punishable by a term of imprisonment exceeding one year? 223

If I plead guilty to a felony, does that mean I was convicted? 224
What if I was convicted of a felony but didn't have an attorney? 225
What if my Felony has been pardoned or expunged? 225
What if I plead nolo contendre to a crime of domestic violence?....................... 226
What if I was convicted of a crime of domestic violence but didn't have an
attorney?... 226
What if my crime of domestic violence has been pardoned or expunged? 227
Removal of a Legal Disability 227
    Eligibility.. 228
    How do I apply for Executive Clemency?... 229
    Application 229
    Certified Copies of Documents 229
    Fees for Certified Documents 230
    Courthouse Security... 230
    Letters of Reference.. 231
    Application Fee.. 231
The Role of the Department 231
Appendix II 233
  Getting the Qualified Non-Resident Form R-168.. 233
    Courthouse Security... 235
Appendix III... 236
  Fingerprints.. 236
About the Authors... 238
About the Legislative Consultant.. 239
Authors' Final Notes... 239

Forward

I spend many hours every week studying gun rights law in South Carolina - both existing law and the new bills being considered by the General Assembly. I frequently appear before House and Senate subcommittees speaking on behalf of gun owners. I also spend a lot of time communicating gun rights issues to my fellow South Carolinians both to stop anti gun rights bills and to support pro gun rights bills.

I am excited about this book because it is so sorely needed. The "legalese" language used in the law is all too often not fully understood by the general public. But, this book is written in easy to understand language along with many examples and even some humor. This book is written specifically for the State of South Carolina but will explain both state and federal laws. It is the only book you will find on South Carolina firearms law, and it is the only one - until it is updated - you will ever need.

Each year Americans use guns over 2 million times in self-defense. This means someone uses a gun to protect him or herself every 13 seconds. But, you seldom hear of the beneficial use of guns in the news. Sometimes you hear a news report about a gun owner who uses his gun but gets sued or arrested. Don't be that guy! Knowledge is power, so read this book.

The money you invest in this book may save you a great deal of money. You can either spend a little on this book or you can buy a lawyer a new yacht with your attorneys' fees. Don't loose your right to own a gun over a careless violation that you don't even know exists. Read this book!

One last reason you should buy this book is because a portion of the proceeds from every book sold goes to the GrassRoots Legal Defense Fund to help pay for the fight to protect your rights.

Robert D. Butler, D.C., J.D.

1

Chapter 1
The Right to Keep and Bear Arms

The Natural Right to Personal Defense

Natural rights are those rights existing outside of any government, constitution or any other institution. The United States Constitution does not create natural rights. Instead, it protects natural rights. The right of an individual to defend against a threat is a natural right and arms are an excellent means to defend against threats of deadly force. The U.S. Constitution specifically protects an individual's natural right to keep and bear arms.

American Character

The ownership and possession of weapons, particularly firearms, is central to the American experience. Since the Pilgrims, Boston Tea Party, and creation of the Constitution, Americans have had firearms.

The Stamp Act angered us, the Declaration of Independence defined us, but a British attempt to confiscate our firearms at Lexington and Concord started the war for independence and freedom. No matter what some egghead college professor in a tweed jacket and penny loafers tells you, guns are an inseparable part of the American character.

Articles of Confederation

The Articles of Confederation predated the United States Constitution. These articles loosely held the states together but they also allowed the states to be autonomous and sovereign.

The Articles provided that the states would maintain well regulated militia as well as sufficient guns and equipment for that militia. Generally the states provided a private right of gun ownership and nowhere did the Articles contradict the states in that regard. Where a state did not specify the right, it was presumed and not challenged.

United States Constitution

In 1791, the Bill of Rights became the law of the land. The Second Amendment guarantees and protects the pre-existing right to keep and bear arms, it does not establish the right. The exact wording is as follows: "A well regulated militia, being necessary to the security of a free state, the right of the people to keep and bear arms, shall not be infringed."

Anti-Individual Gun Rights Obfuscation

Anti-individual gun rights activists sometimes get away with obfuscating the plain meaning of the Second Amendment. They say that it only guarantees the right to a well regulated militia and not an individual right to have guns. However, this exact issue was discussed during the Articles of Confederation.[1] During those debates, the liberal obfuscation was explicitly rejected. The anti-individual gun rights obfuscation is a twisted argument positing that the Second Amendment only means that States can have a "well regulated militia" but that individuals do not have a right to keep or bear arms.

Historical Context of the Second Amendment

The Second Amendment does not specifically say that we have a right to be provided with a well regulated militia. It does, on the other hand, presume that a militia is a requirement of any free state. By implication, this means that the framers of the Constitution intended for us to have a well regulated militia. When the Constitution was written, militias were made up of all citizens who had a gun and knew how to use it. The overall number of members in the combined colonial militias was much greater than that of the professional military. During the early part of the Revolutionary War, the only troops existing were groups of ordinary armed citizens who organized militias. The colonists had no regular professional military as we know it today.

---

[1] Dowlut, Robert, The Right to Keep and Bear Arms: A Right to Self-Defense Against Criminals and Despots, Stanford L. & Pol'y Rev. 25-40, 1977.

The key concept to the militias was the lack of government control. The militias were regulated, but that regulation was done internally. Members voted for the leaders of their individual militias. Everyone was a volunteer and could leave at any time and there was no funding from any level of government. As a result, the government did not control the militia.

The founders envisioned a nation run by the people. They wanted the people to have the power and not the government. Towards this aim, the founders thought it critical to keep the populace armed as a fighting force to discourage and repel a tyrannical home front government as well as foreign invaders. Notice there are two purposes of the armed populace.

Anti-individual gun rights activists claim that there is no need for armed citizens because we now have the military branches and National Guard. Notice however that the militia is entirely different from the military branches and National Guard. The National Guard is funded by the government. The government makes the rules and chooses the leaders. The members of the National Guard are not free to leave until dismissed. The fact that the National Guard is funded and controlled by government makes it ineffective at dispensing with a tyrannical government. Therefore, we still need an armed populace to do this job, should it become necessary.

Additional Support of the Right

A full discussion of the Second Amendment is beyond the scope of this book. Numerous resources are available for individual study of the subject. Simple searches on the internet or at your local library should provide you with a good start. The authors encourage you to always be ready to defend this vital right.

Current Activity of the United States Supreme Court

The United States Supreme Court has just published the most important Second Amendment opinion in its history. The last time that the Supreme Court even examined the Second Amendment was <u>United States v. Miller</u> in 1939.

<u>U.S. v. Miller</u> was generally seen as flawed and inconclusive because it did not address the right to keep and bear arms directly and the government's case before the Supreme Court went uncontested. What remains remarkable about <u>U.S. v. Miller</u> is it was one of the rare times that the Supreme Court even mulled-over the extent of private gun rights. Being second only to the right to religion and free speech, giving the Second Amendment such short-shrift can be viewed as inexcusable neglect.

Fortunately, the current majority of the Court believes in individual rights and the role of the Constitution in protecting those rights from the government. In <u>D.C. v. Heller</u>, (2008), an individual challenged a District of Columbia law that prevented a resident from keeping functioning firearms in their home. Heller had asked the Court to determine whether the Second Amendment protects the natural right of law-abiding, adult individuals to keep ordinary, functional firearms, including handguns, in their homes.

In a 5-4 decision, the Supreme Court recognized that the Second Amendment does protect an individual's right to keep a functioning handgun in their home. The decision explains, in depth, the difference between an individual right and one which is tied to a collective organization like a militia. The court rejected the argument that the right to keep and bear arms is tied to service in the military or in some militia.

The court looked closely at the two phrases of the Second Amendment that we have already discussed, "A well regulated Militia, being necessary to the security of a free state (first phrase)," and, "the right of the people to keep and bear arms, shall not be infringed (second phrase)." The court said that the first phrase does not limit the second one. The first phrase only explains the reason the second phrase is important.

The Court also recognized that the right to use arms for self-defense and other lawful purposes is inherent in the Second Amendment. The decision also recognized that the right to keep and bear arms was a right that existed before our country was established. If you remember the words of the Declaration of Independence, "endowed by their Creator with certain unalienable rights," the Court basically found the right to keep and bear arms as one of these unalienable rights. So the right to keep and bear arms is greater than a right created by laws or the government. Instead, it is an inherent right that exists on its own. The only role of the Constitution is to protect that right from the government.

In summary, the Supreme Court recognizes the existing individual right to keep and bear arms in one's home for lawful purposes including self-defense. This Supreme Court decision is monumental for gun owners and should be celebrated as one of the great landmark decisions.

Gun owners should also remember that the decision might have been very different several years ago. The 5-4 decision would not have been possible but for the recent confirmation of two judges (Roberts and Alito) who were nominated by a President who promised judges that would strictly interpret the Constitution and not legislate from the bench. Gun owners are well advised to consider all candidates for office and elect those who will nominate only judges who understand that their role is to faithfully apply the law as written, not impose their opinions through judicial fiat.

The South Carolina Constitution

In addition to the guarantees provided for in the United States Constitution, the Constitution of the State of South Carolina also guarantees the right to bear arms. The exact wording of Article I Section 20 provides, "A well regulated militia being necessary to the security of a free state, the right of the people to keep and bear arms shall not be infringed." The astute reader will notice that, with the exception of two omitted commas, the South Carolina Constitution uses exactly the same words as the United State Constitution. The same analysis is applicable to it as is applicable to the Second Amendment to the United States' Constitution.

The Police Power of the States

Much of the gun and weapons law that you will need to know comes from the South Carolina Code of Laws. The state derives authority to regulate firearms through its implicit *police power*. The term police power is basically legal slang and not very illustrative of the real nature of the power. Often, the term makes people think of police officers. A more correct terminology would be *policy* power. A state can make policies that provide for the health, safety, and welfare of its residents. State policy is codified in the statutes (South Carolina Code of Laws) and the regulations (Code of Regulations) that implement those statutes.

The policy power of states is generally the strongest power that a state has. Courts historically give great deference to state attempts to provide for the health, safety and welfare of its residents. A court will find a statute or regulation constitutional if the state can show virtually any rational basis for enacting the law. For instance, if the legislature and governor determine that wearing dress shoes causes excessive wear to sidewalks, the state can pass a law that prohibits the use of dress shoes in the state.

Where the state runs into limitations on its policy power is when a statute or regulation infringes upon fundamental rights. Fundamental rights are rights that are so important that they deserve special protection. Examples of fundamental rights are voting, worship, political speech, and bearing arms. If a statute or regulation infringes upon a fundamental right, courts will require the state to have a compelling reason for the law and to prove that there is no less restrictive way to accomplish the goal of the legislation. This has historically been a very high hurdle for states to overcome. Therefore, laws that infringe upon fundamental rights are generally struck down by the courts as unconstitutional.

The South Carolina Code of Laws

Using its policy power, South Carolina regulates guns, weapons, ammunition, and explosives through the Code of Laws. Executive agencies such as SLED and the South Carolina Department of Natural Resources implement the Code of Laws with regulations. Finally, executive departments such as the Highway Patrol and various police and sheriff's offices execute and enforce the Code of Laws and regulations.

County and Municipal Home Rule Power

South Carolina is a home rule state. This means that local governments like counties, cities, and special districts are free to make their own local legislation and regulations for their own health, safety and welfare. However, where the state regulates a subject area or specifically prohibits a local government from regulating a subject area, the local government must subordinate itself to state law.

State Law Trumps Local Ordinances

Since the South Carolina legislature has chosen to regulate the subject area of guns, weapons, and ammunition, local governments are not free to make laws that contradict or otherwise impair the state statutes and regulations. Section 23-31-510 of the South Carolina Code of Laws provides that, "No governing body of any county, municipality, or other political subdivision in this State may enact or promulgate any regulation or ordinance which regulates or attempts to regulate the transfer, ownership, possession, carrying, or transportation of firearms, ammunition, components of firearms, or any combination of these things." What this means is that your local government cannot make any laws or regulations that affect virtually anything related to guns. Therefore, if your local government makes a law or policy that contradicts the state statutes, you can bring that law before a court and it will likely be found in violation of state statutes.

Be aware, however, that the state statutes do allow local governments to pass laws that deal with the discharge of firearms, public brandishing of firearms, and brandishing of firearms in connection with major disruptions of order such as riots, insurrections, and during natural disasters. In the case of State v. Johnson, decided in 1907, the South Carolina Supreme Court rejected a constitutionality challenge to a Charleston ordinance prohibiting the discharge of firearms within the city limits. The court reasoned that the ordinance did not prohibit an individual from possessing a firearm on his or her premises, but merely prohibited him or her from discharging the gun within the city limits. Therefore, the ordinance was a reasonable exercise of the city's police power.

Confiscation of Firearms

Further, South Carolina Code of Laws Section 23-31-520 prohibits a local government from confiscating firearms or ammunition unless the confiscation comes incident to an arrest. This law is a required reaction to recent government abuses such as police being ordered to confiscate citizens' guns during the Hurricane Katrina emergency.

Conclusion

The Second Amendment to the Constitution of the United States provides that Americans have a right to keep and bear arms. By a narrow 5-4 decision, the United States Supreme Court has recently held that the right to keep and bear arms is fundamental. However, there are many who seek to diminish this right.

The South Carolina Constitution recognizes the right to keep and bear arms. The State of South Carolina regulates guns, weapons, and ammunition under its inherent policy power. Finally, South Carolina local governments are prohibited from enacting virtually any law that regulates guns, weapons or ammunition.

Chapter 2
Legal Requirements for Buying a Gun and Ammunition

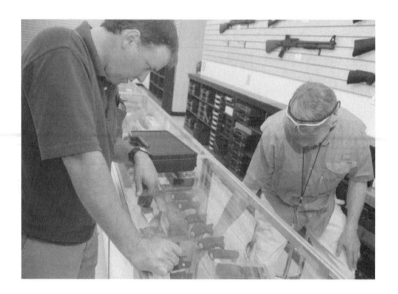

Merchants that have been in business for any length of time will tell you that the first qualification for buying something is that you have enough money. Modern merchants will tell you that there is an exception to this if you have enough credit on your credit card. Anyway, now that the obvious qualifications are out of the way, let's get to the legal requirements for buying a gun.

Gun Sellers

You will read the term Federal Firearms License or "FFL." This term means a person or business that has a federally issued license to sell or transfer guns. Generally we are talking about retail gun shops and sporting goods stores but there are many FFL holders who can legally sell guns outside of stores and shops. If you are not buying from a gun shop or retail sporting goods store, you should be extra careful to read this chapter and know that you are dealing with a person you can trust.

Age for Purchasing from a Federally Licensed Dealer

In order to legally purchase a legal rifle or shotgun from a person or business with a federal firearms dealer's license, you must be at least 18 years of age. This age requirement also applies to ammunition for the rifle or shotgun. In other words, you must be 18 years of age to purchase the gun or the ammunition from a federally licensed dealer. This is federal law.

While the general rule is that you have to be at least 18 years of age to purchase a rifle, shotgun or ammunition from a dealer, you must be at least 21 years of age to purchase a **handgun** from a federally licensed dealer. Remember that this same rule also applies to handgun ammunition if you are purchasing it from a dealer. Complicating this is that certain types of ammunition are used in both handguns and rifles. The .22 caliber long rifle is a good example. Other examples include the .45 ACP, .44 magnum, and 9 millimeter parabellum. If you tell the dealer that you are buying these calibers to use in a rifle, but really intend to use it for a handgun, the store might sell it to you. However, you have just committed a Federal crime by lying about what you will use the ammunition for. So if you really plan to use that .22 long rifle ammunition in a handgun, keep a good $10,000 in cash on hand with you for bail and a good criminal attorney.

If you lie about your age or any other fact on your application to purchase a gun, you are committing a crime. The same is true if you use a fake identification. You can be prosecuted under United States Code

Section 922 for using false information or a fake ID to purchase a gun. Maybe you have a slick fake ID that got you into the bars in high school or college. Don't even think of using it to buy a gun. If you get caught trying to drink with a fake ID, chances are they just take your ID. If you try to buy a *handgun* with false information or a fake ID, you can be charged for a felony that carries a penalty of up to 5 years in jail, up to $2,000 fine, or both and that devastating felony record (South Carolina Code of Laws Section 23-31-160).

Age Requirement for Purchase from Private Individual

As a result of an amendment to Section 16-23-30, South Carolina Code of Laws, on April 2, 2008, 18 year olds can now buy a handgun from a private (non-FFL-licensed) individual. (Remember, a person still has to be 21 years old to buy a handgun from a federally licensed dealer). This amended statute also allows an 18 year old to be given or possess a handgun.

What does it mean to purchase from an individual? An individual can be a neighbor or someone selling at a gun show. It can also mean someone who is selling a gun in the classified ads. What the seller cannot be is a dealer as defined by the FFL regulations. As a general rule, the local gun shop will be run by an FFL holder. Be on the lookout at gun shows because many of the sellers are FFL holders and these federally licensed dealers cannot sell handguns to anyone under 21 years of age. (They probably don't want to anyway but just be careful.)

What about 18 year olds buying ammunition? Again, federally licensed firearms dealers cannot sell handgun ammunition to anyone under 21 years of age. As to non-FFL ammunition sellers, no controlling legal authority is apparent so you are in a legal grey area. Proceed with caution if you are under 21 years old and trying to buy handgun ammunition.

It is important to note that the concealed weapons permit statute and rules have not changed with the handgun age amendment. Therefore, an applicant still must be 21 years of age to be considered for a concealed weapons permit. So, as of now, the only way that someone under 21 years can legally carry or transport a handgun is under the non-concealed weapons permit rules explained in Chapter 6 of this book.

Residency

Federal law prohibits the sale of a firearm by someone who does not have a federal firearm's license to any person who is not a resident of the state where the transfer takes place. There is an exception to this rule in cases of temporary transfers. The same federal law also prohibits sales to non-residents by federal licensees except under the following circumstances:

- Temporary transfers. This means that you can loan or rent a gun to a non-resident. The temporary transfer must be for a lawful sporting purpose like hunting or target shooting.

- Inheritance. This means that a non-resident can receive a gun through bequest or devise upon the death of the owner.

- Face-to-Face Transaction. In other words, the gun being sold is a shotgun or rifle, the purchase is from a federal licensee and the transaction is done face-to-face. This means no mail order, no internet, and no ordering by calling over the phone.

You can buy a handgun or a long gun from a federally licensed dealer in another state if all four of the following are in place:

- The dealer must transfer the gun to a federally licensed dealer in your state.

- Your dealer in South Carolina must send a copy of his license to the dealer in the other state.

- Gun dealer, gun sale and gun purchase laws of both states must be completely followed.

- Form 4473 is completely filled out when you pick up the gun.

 If you buy from an out of state dealer, the dealer will send the gun directly to your South Carolina dealer and your South Carolina dealer will deliver possession to you in South Carolina.

Must be a Resident or Military to Buy a Pistol from a Dealer

On top of federal law, South Carolina Code of Laws Section 23-31-140 makes it a felony for non-South Carolina residents to purchase a pistol in the state from a "dealer." This law makes no distinctions about whether the seller holds an FFL or not. So, one who attempts or actually purchases from a dealer is subject to this residency requirement.

Possessing a valid South Carolina driver's license or Department of Motor Vehicles identification card is enough proof of residency.

Military personnel on active duty in possession of a current United States military identification card need not be residents under this Section. However, don't forget the federal prohibitions discussed above for purchases from an FFL. The penalty for violating this law is a fine up to $2,000, prison for up to 5 years or both.

"Dealer" is defined in South Carolina Code of Laws Section 23-31-110(b) as any person engaged in the business of selling firearms at retail or any person who is a pawnbroker. It is unclear if "at retail" is defined as any or all gun show tables. If it is all gun show tables, a non-resident is prohibited from purchasing a pistol from a gun show table even if the seller is merely offering his private collection for sale. We did not find case law defining dealer so you are cautioned accordingly at gun shows. Alternatively, someone selling a pistol from their private collection at their home is almost certainly not retail (unless they are running a retail business, or something close to it, from their home).

Dealers Cannot Deal in Handguns Made from Certain Metals

South Carolina has a statutory provision against "dealers" dealing in pistols or other handguns that are manufactured with certain metals (South Carolina Code of Laws Section 23-31-180). The stated theory is that guns made from metals that melt at low temperatures are unsafe. However, it is reasonable to infer that the law was created to limit the availability of inexpensive guns that would be more easily afforded by criminals or younger purchasers.

It is a felony, with the penalty of up to 5 years in jail, up to $2,000 fine, or both for a dealer to hold, store, handle, sell, offer for sale, or otherwise possess in his place of business, any pistol which has a die-cast, metal alloy frame or receiver, which melts at a temperature of less than 800 degrees Fahrenheit is illegal contraband. Again, "dealer" is defined in South Carolina Code of Laws Section 23-31-110(b) as any person engaged in the business of selling firearms at retail or any person who is a pawnbroker.

In addition, law enforcement will seize any such weapon from you. You are provided an opportunity for hearing on the materials, manufacture and quality of the gun. However, if the gun is found in violation of the South Carolina Code of Laws, the gun will be confiscated. Thereafter, the confiscating agency can either destroy it, dispose of it, keep it and use it within their department, transfer it to another department, or render it inoperable and use it for display purposes. They must also keep a record of all confiscated pistols. If you suspect one of these guns at a retail dealer, the best advice is to avoid buying such a gun from that dealer.

Inheritance

Weapons can be transferred through a will. Individuals, including minors, can take title to firearms though inheritance. Even machine guns can be inherited. For more information about transferring machine guns through inheritance, see the chapter on Weapon Crimes and Lawsuits. If you are interested in transferring a firearm through a will or if you are concerned about the legality of an inherited firearm, see an estate planning attorney familiar with firearms inheritance.

NFA Machine Gun Trust

Machine guns and similar weapons that are regulated under the National Firearms Act NFA (discussed later in the book) can be acquired and owned by a special trust designed to own the weapon. The trustee of the trust can keep and use the weapon just as if he owns it in his or her name. The main reason for the growing popularity of such trusts is because the NFA generally requires approval by the local sheriff or comparable law enforcement chief. This can be an insurmountable challenge if your particular chief does not want you to have an NFA regulated weapon. While the trust itself is relatively straight forward, the consultation and advice of an attorney is critical in acting under the trust and determining heirs. Therefore, do not attempt one of these trusts on your own. Instead, seek counsel from an attorney that knows NFA gun trusts.

Registration of Guns

Finally, there is no registration of guns in South Carolina nor is there a federal law that requires you to register a gun with some agency. Therefore, once you acquire your typical pistol, rifle or shotgun, you are not required to register it with the government. However, fully automatic, machine guns, and other weapons regulated under the National Firearms Act (NFA) require a type of registration.

Conclusion

There are laws that must be followed when purchasing a gun. Make sure that you understand the law before purchasing a gun so that you do not end up with a criminal record or jail time. Do not rely solely on the gun seller, especially if the seller is not a reputable local gun shop. Always know the law for yourself.

Summary Points

- You must be at least 18 years old to buy a rifle or shotgun and any ammunition for these firearms.

- You must be at least 21 years old to buy a handgun or ammunition for a handgun from a federally licensed (FFL) dealer.

- Some ammunition can be used in both handguns and rifles. If you are under 21, don't buy ammunition if you intend to use it in a handgun.

- A person 18 years of older can buy, legally obtain, and possess a handgun if obtained from a private seller or person that resides in the same state as the 18 year old person. (i.e. the 18 year old person can not get a handgun from his uncle who lives in another state unless first transferred through an FFL to a 21 year old person who lives in the 18 year old person's state of residence and the 21 year old transfers it to the 18 year old.)

- Generally, a dealer can not sell a gun to someone who is not a resident of the state in which the sale is made. However, there are some exceptions to this general rule.

Chapter 3
Legal Disabilities and Executive Clemency

What is a Legal Disability?

A legal disability is a personal condition that prevents you from lawfully purchasing or possessing a gun. Legal disabilities can arise from a criminal record, mental condition, or certain other misconduct that the government deems problematic. If you have a legal disability, it is a crime for you to sell, transfer, possess, or receive a firearm.

What is the Lifetime Federal Firearms Disability?

Those with federal or state felony conviction or adjudication, or those with a federal misdemeanor conviction with a *potential* jail term of more than 1 year, or those with a state misdemeanor conviction that carries the *potential* jail term of greater than 2 years, virtually always have a legal disability. Notice that the word <u>potential</u> is italicized. That is because the law does care about the actual sentence applied. The federal firearms disability engages based upon the potential penalty of a given offense as opposed to the actual sentence handed-down by a judge or negotiated with the prosecutor. For a more detailed discussion of the lifetime federal firearms disability and removal of a legal disability, see *Appendix I*.

So, expanding upon the general rule above, you have a legal disability if one of the following applies to you:

- you were convicted or adjudicated for a federal or South Carolina felony; or you were convicted or adjudicated of a federal misdemeanor with a *potential* jail term of greater than 1 year or a South Carolina misdemeanor with a *potential* jail term of greater than 2 years;

- you were convicted of a felony or another state's misdemeanor with a *potential* jail term of greater than 2 years;

- you are under indictment or information for a federal or state felony, a federal misdemeanor crime with a *potential* jail term more than 1 year, or a state misdemeanor with a *potential* jail term of more than 2 years. However, this might not rule-out possession of a firearm until a sentence is imposed; or

- you are fleeing another state to avoid prosecution for a crime or avoid testifying in a criminal proceeding.

Second, certain mental conditions can impute a legal disability. Therefore, you have a legal disability if one of the following applies to you:

- you are addicted to or using illegal drugs (this is true even if you are only occasionally using marijuana or other "recreational" drugs);

- you have been adjudicated mentally defective, or are committed to a mental institution, or have been committed to a mental institution sometime in the past.

  Commitment to a mental institution means the involuntary placement in a mental facility after some legitimate board, agency or court of mental illness determines that you have a mental defect that requires involuntary treatment. Involuntary commitment for drug or alcohol use is included in this definition.

  Note though, if you had been placed in a mental facility, against your will, for the purpose of observation of your suspected condition, such commitment would not count against you. Only after you have been determined to have a mental defect that requires involuntary admission to a mental facility would a legal disability arise. Voluntary admission to a mental facility is not included. So, by all means, if you think that you have some mental condition, worry about seeing a doctor first and worry about how it will affect your gun rights later; or

- you have been found not guilty by reason of insanity in a criminal case.

Unfortunately, some Vietnam Era and other veterans are being denied their right to keep and bear arms under some language in the Veterans Disarmament Act of 2007. This controversial and hastily passed federal law has the effect of allowing some diagnoses of post traumatic stress disorder to satisfy the *adjudicated mentally defective* standard discussed above. A full discussion of the Veterans Disarmament Act is beyond the scope of this book but affected veterans should consult with an attorney to assist in removing a legal disability caused by the Act.

Finally, miscellaneous misconduct or other circumstances can impute you with a legal disability. Therefore, you have a legal disability if one of the following applies to you:

- you were dishonorably discharged from military service;

- you renounce your U.S. citizenship;

- you are subject to a domestic restraining order where the court found you a credible threat to the physical safety of another. Alternatively, that the court order expressly prohibits the use, threatened or attempted use of physical force; or

- you were convicted of a misdemeanor crime of domestic violence as defined in 18 USC 922(g)(9). Generally this means an offense that involves the attempted use of physical force, or the threatened use of a deadly weapon, committed by a current or former spouse, parent, or guardian of the victim, by a person with whom the victim shares a child in common, by a person who is cohabiting with or has cohabited with the victim as a spouse, parent, or guardian, or by a person similarly situated to a spouse, parent, or guardian of the victim. It doesn't apply to casual relationships unless you were living together. Under current federal law it likely includes cases where a "guilty" plea was entered vs. "no contest" plea, or where there was a trial with a "guilty" verdict, even if adjudication was later "withheld." It will always include an "adjudication" of guilt.

The Legal Danger of Domestic Violence

If you have a domestic violence conviction, federal law provides some instances where your legal disability can be removed. For example, if your conviction occurred when you were not represented by an attorney, and where you did not knowingly and voluntarily waive your right to an attorney. Likewise, if you were entitled to a jury trial, and did not knowingly or intelligently waive that right, you might be able to have your legal disability removed. Further, if you are able to get a pardon you might be able to have your legal disability removed. If you think that you might legitimately be able to raise one of these defenses, go see a criminal, civil rights or firearms attorney. Do not try to fix this type of disability yourself.

You should be getting the picture that it is very difficult for someone implicated in domestic violence to legally possess a gun or get a concealed weapons permit. Stay clear of even a hint of domestic violence. First and foremost, there is no reason to solve interpersonal problems by battering or physically threatening someone. Second, society does not want people with an uncontrolled temper around deadly weapons. Therefore, if you have an anger problem or are prone to domestic violence, please get some help with your emotions before you ruin your chance to legally possess or conceal a firearm.

How Do I Remove a Legal Disability?

If you have a legal disability, there are steps that you can take to have it removed. *Appendix I* of this book discusses the steps that you must take to seek removal.

Summary Points

- A legal disability is a personal condition that prevents you from lawfully purchasing or possessing a gun.

- A legal disability can arise from a conviction of a crime, a mental condition, or certain miscellaneous misconduct or circumstances.

Chapter 4
Concealed Weapons Permit

Introduction

Every once in a while, a law is passed that actually helps the average citizen. South Carolina's concealed weapons law helps you protect yourself and others from deadly attacks. The law provides for a permitting system that gives private citizens a license to carry firearms in public.

What Does the Permit Allow?

Generally, the permit allows you to carry a handgun around with you to most places. Specifically, the statute says that a permit holder can carry a concealable weapon, in a concealed manner, in certain places under certain circumstances. These terms will be defined in this chapter.

What does Concealable Weapon Mean?

Concealable weapon is defined as a firearm having a length of less than twelve inches measured along its greatest dimension. The statute talks about firearms and no other weapons. Also, the statute limits the overall length to **less than** twelve inches. So, for all intents and purposes, the statute basically allows the permit holder to conceal small and medium sized handguns.

As a point of reference, small .38 Special caliber revolvers are usually about six or seven inches in overall length. Both the Ruger LCP and Kel-Tec .380 caliber pistols are about five and one-half inches long. These guns are all well under twelve inches long and are firearms so they would be legal for a concealed weapons permit holder to carry. The Smith & Wesson 327 Night Guard revolver in .357 magnum caliber is nearly eight inches in overall length. The Magnum Research Mark XIX Desert Eagle automatic pistol chambered in .357 magnum caliber is a little more than ten and one-half inches long. These guns are also well under twelve inches long and are firearms so they would be legal for a concealed weapons permit holder to carry.

On the other hand, Kel-Tec manufactures the PLR-16 Pistol. This firearm is configured like a pistol but is chambered in the .223 Remington rifle round and is over eighteen inches in overall length. This pistol is a firearm but is over eighteen inches in overall length so it does not meet the statutory definition of concealable weapon.

Those who have seen the Clint Eastwood Dirty Harry movies know that he carried a Smith & Wesson revolver chambered in the .44 magnum caliber. While there is some debate, most tend to agree that Dirty Harry was carrying a Model 29. The current Smith & Wesson Model 29 revolver is chambered in .44 magnum and has an overall length of exactly twelve inches. The statute defines concealable weapon as less than twelve inches in overall length. Therefore, if Dirty Harry was an ordinary South Carolina resident with a concealed weapons permit, he would not be able to carry his famous .44 magnum revolver concealed (nor could he carry it openly). Knowing Dirty Harry, he would follow the law and not carry the handgun even if he was "feelin' lucky" that day. Dirty Harry knows that criminal gun charges will not, "make his day."

What does Concealed Mean?

Concealed is defined as, "carried in a manner that is hidden from public view in normal wearing of clothing." If a handgun is in a holster inside of your belt and fully concealed by your pants and shirt, it is concealed by your clothes. If it is fully inside of your jeans front pocket, it is concealed by your clothes. If it is in an ankle holster and covered by your slacks, it is concealed by your clothes. However, if it is stuck halfway in your back pocket and you wear a shirt that is not designed to drop down below your back pocket, the gun is not concealed by your clothing. Similarly, if you walk around with a pistol in a holster on the outside of your hip, it is not concealed by your clothes.

Notice that we keep mentioning the idea of concealment by your clothes. The permit requires that your concealable weapon be concealed by your clothes in the normal wearing of clothes. Therefore, if you are wearing an article of clothing in the manner in which it was designed to be worn, and you are able to conceal your weapon with that article of clothing, you are concealing the weapon as contemplated in the statute. (It should be noted that a woman's purse and man's briefcase are considered articles of clothing for the purposes of the statute.)

As an example, say that you have a holster that holds a pistol in the small of your back. The pistol is concealed from public view by the normal wearing of your shirt. While in a store though, you reach high for a box and the shirt rides up your back above the pistol. As a result, a patron on the aisle sees the pistol on your back and calls the police. It can be argued that you have not violated the law because the shirt was designed to hang over the small of the back. Alternatively, the prosecution can argue that you have violated the law because reaching for a box in a store is normal activity and your gun should therefore have remained concealed. So, the best practice is to always insure that your clothing conceals the weapon even in situations like reaching high up on a shelf. Keeping the weapon concealed might prevent an unnecessary charge and a jury determining your fate.

What Does the Permit NOT Allow?

The permit does not deputize you as a citizen's auxiliary police officer. A permit holder should not consider him or herself a law enforcement officer. Likewise, he or she should not act as an armed vigilante. The permit is designed to allow the holder to carry a weapon in case it is needed to repel a deadly or great bodily harm attack. More details of where you can carry a concealable weapon, concealed, with the permit will follow later in this chapter. Initially though, we will explain how to get the permit.

Qualifications

First, you must be either a resident of the State of South Carolina or a qualified non-resident. The term "resident" means that you intend to make South Carolina your permanent home for now. It also includes military personnel permanently stationed in South Carolina. If you are not a resident you can still get a permit if you are a qualified non-resident. Qualified Non-resident means that you reside in a state other than South Carolina but you own real estate in South Carolina.

Additionally, you must be at least 21 years of age. This might be an area ripe for a court challenge because 18 year olds can already possess a handgun and the South Carolina Supreme Court has already ruled that it is unconstitutional to deny 18 year old adults the right to keep and bear arms. Further, 18 year olds can buy a handgun from a private (non-FFL-licensed) individual. The legislature should create a permit that fills this gap. However, for now, you must be at least 21 to get the permit.

Also, you must not suffer from a physical infirmity that would prevent you from passing the range qualification portion of the concealed weapons permit course. Alternatively, you must not suffer from a physical infirmity that would prevent you from completing one of the alternate proofs of training discussed later in this chapter. Finally, you must be able to legally own or possess weapons as detailed in the chapters on legal requirements for buying a gun and legal disabilities.

The Application Process

Obtaining a concealed weapons permit is a fairly simple process. You must provide a complete and accurate application and provide proof of training. SLED has created a checklist for completion of the application on their website.

You can save a tremendous amount of time, energy and hassle by signing-up for your required training with an instructor that provides most of the other application requirements also. In other words, some training instructors and programs offer only the training while others

 offer the complete service of application, fingerprints, pictures, etc. It is a great convenience to have all of the application requirements assembled by your instructor on the day of your concealed weapons permit class. For a list of instructors, see the SC GrassRoots GunRights website at SCFirearms.org.

The Application Form

However, if you want to apply on your own, you get started by fully completing a South Carolina Concealed Weapons Permit Application Form R-078 (Revised 9/15/06). The application form itself is available to the public through the South Carolina Law Enforcement Department (SLED). The most efficient way to get an application is to simply download and print one from your computer. Go to SLED's website at: www.sled.sc.gov and click on "Concealed Weapons Permit Program" on the left side of the website and thereafter click on "Concealed Weapons Permit Application." The application can be downloaded in .doc format. You can get a hard copy of the application mailed to you by calling SLED headquarters in Columbia at: (803) 737-9000. You can also mail a request for an application directly to SLED at: P.O. Box 21398, Columbia, SC, 29221. If you are requesting an application by mail, you might want to call SLED first to see if they require that you provide a self-addressed, stamped envelope.

The application requires that you give your name, date of birth, place of birth, sex, race, height, weight, eye color, hair color, current residence address (if you are a qualified non-resident you will also have to give the address of the property that you own in the state), and all residence addresses for the three years prior to the application. (We will talk about proof of residency or qualified non-residency a little later in this chapter). Additionally, you must certify that you are not prohibited from possessing a weapon under state law. You must also certify that you understand that, should you later become prohibited from possessing a weapon, your permit is automatically revoked and you must surrender it immediately to SLED. Further, you must certify that you are a resident of South Carolina or that you are a qualified non-resident. If you choose to qualify through a SLED approved instructor, there is a place on the form where your training instructor must certify that you completed the requisite training. Alternatively, if you choose to qualify through one of the alternatives to the class for proof of training, you will need to provide the proper documentation. Finally, you must then certify that all of the information that you have provided is true and correct to the best of your knowledge.

Arrests, Pleas, Convictions and Traffic Tickets

One of the questions asks: *Have you **ever** pled guilty, been found guilty, paid a fine, forfeited bond, been jailed or placed on probation for any offense? If yes, furnish details on another sheet.* Look to the reverse side of the application for more instructions as to this question. Yes, they do mean "ever. . . " Put down any run-ins with the law that you may have had. If you do not, the background check will probably find them. If you are found to be dishonest on the application, SLED has a reason to prevent you from ever getting a permit in South Carolina. So, if you bought beer for your friends 25 years ago and got caught, put it down. If you got in a fight back in your military days, put it down. If you ever had any run-in with the criminal legal system, put it down.

This means traffic (moving violation) tickets also. Fortunately though, it does not appear that SLED is requiring that you itemize every traffic violation. If you have ever had a traffic violation, it appears that SLED will accept that you answer the question "yes" and then write (in the space under the question), "I have traffic violations." Be aware that there have been applicants who were initially denied for failing to list traffic offenses. These applicants were later granted a permit after subsequently providing a listing of the traffic offenses but SLED could have used the omission to permanently prevent the applicants from obtaining a permit.

Be aware of SLED's rule (explained on the reverse of the application) regarding the number of traffic violations. If you have **ever** had six (6) traffic violations within **any** five (5) year period, SLED can use that for a basis of denial. If you have had six or more traffic violations within a five year span, report those violations to SLED on a separate sheet of paper.

This is a good time to emphasize the importance of reading the official instructions on the reverse side of the application. In addition to any last minute requirements that have been imposed since the printing of this book, there is also a very helpful checklist to make sure that you have your application in order before sending it off. If you get your application from the internet, these instructions will print as a separate page.

Residency and Proof of Residency

You must also submit proof of residency or qualified non-residency. First, let's figure-out if you are a resident, qualified nonresident, or a non-resident. Remember, permits are only legal for residents and qualified non-residents.

Resident

In general, you are a resident if you live in South Carolina and are not just visiting. A South Carolina driver's license is good evidence that you "live" in South Carolina. If you live close to a bordering state, it is not a problem that you work or otherwise have significant contacts with the neighboring state. Primarily, the South Carolina Code of Laws and SLED are interested in your physical residence.

Military Resident

There is one additional classification of resident. If you are a member of the military of the United States and are stationed in South Carolina or on permanent change of station orders, you qualify as a resident. Remember, if you get stationed somewhere out of South Carolina, you should forfeit your permit to SLED.

For residents and military residents, you must send a (non-certified) photocopy of your driver's license or an official identification card issued by the South Carolina Department of Motor Vehicles. The Form does not require a notary to verify any information on the photocopy of your identification. You can alternately send a photocopy of the following: voter's registration card, South Carolina Department of Revenue ID, any state or federal law enforcement agency ID, US Department of Defense ID, or US State Department ID. It can also be satisfied by the presentation of a certified copy of any other document which SLED determines satisfies the requirement. If you have a document other than a South Carolina Driver's License or SCDMV Identification Card, always contact SLED first to see if they will accept it. Even if they say yes on the phone, there is no guarantee that they will actually accept it with your application. Why not just give them an SC driver's license or SCDMV identification card in the first place? No need to reinvent the wheel here unless absolutely necessary.

Non-US Citizens

There are special requirements for residents who are non-US citizens. Additionally, non-US citizens must mark additional boxes on the Form R-078. Discussing the requirements for non-US citizens is beyond the scope of this book and those applicants are encouraged to have an attorney assist them with the application.

Qualified Non-Resident

If you do not reside in South Carolina, you can still get a permit if you qualify as a *qualified non-resident*. To meet this qualification, you must own real estate in South Carolina. Ownership means that you must have, at least, a partial legal ownership interest. So, for example, if you live in Alabama but you inherited a ¼ interest in a parcel of land in Pickens from your great grandfather, you can apply as a qualified non-resident.

As proof of ownership of South Carolina real estate, you must submit a completed and signed SLED Form R-168 (South Carolina Non-Resident Concealed Weapon Permit (CWP) Real Property Tax

Form). This form must be completed by the county assessor of the county in which the property is located in South Carolina. This completed form verifies your ownership. You can obtain the form online at SLED's website: www.sled.sc.gov, or by calling SLED at: (803) 896-7014. You must also send SLED a photocopy of your valid out-of-state driver's license, DMV issued ID card or other ID from the list described in the previous section for residents.

SLED has issued permit cards for qualified non-residents that are not the same dimensions and quality as the resident card. (The card traditionally issued to residents is the same size and quality as a South Carolina driver's license.) Qualified non-residents may be issued a $4^{5/8}$ inch wide by $2^{7/8}$ inch high card. Those dimensions are considerably larger than the regular permit card and are not within the statutory parameters of 3½ inches by 3 inches (South Carolina Code of Law Section 23-31-215(A). Further, the qualified non-resident cards appear to have been simply printed from a color desktop printer. The photo provided with the application is then cut with scissors and the entire card is hand-laminated. Overall, the qualified non-resident card is bulky and does not look like a permit issued by a governmental entity. It looks homemade and does not fit in a standard wallet.

SLED personnel have indicated that the agency simply does not have the funding to produce a statutorily compliant permit card. While a lack of funding is not a legal excuse for failing to comply with the statute, SLED will likely to continue to issue the illegally large card until challenged by an administrator, lawsuit or public pressure.

Getting Qualified Non-Resident Paperwork from Government Offices

If you are a qualified non-resident, your completed SLED Form R-168 must be signed by the county assessor in which your South Carolina property is located. Please refer to Appendix II for additional information about getting this paperwork.

Photographs

If you are a resident, SLED's practice has been to electronically import South Carolina driver's license pictures into the new concealed weapons permits. Therefore, the picture on resident's concealed weapons permits is the exact same digital picture that appears on the driver's license. That being said, **all** applicants still must provide SLED with a copy of his drivers license or SLED-accepted ID in the application package.

You must include a color photograph of your full face. The picture should be of your face and neck only. The statutes indicate that it cannot be any smaller than one inch high and one inch wide (1" by 1") and no larger than three inches by five inches (3" X 5"). While the statutes do not specifically prohibit it, we recommend against sending a photocopy of your picture. If you are handy with computers, you can get away with sending in a good quality digital photograph printed from your own color printer. If you do so, make sure that you use photographic quality printing paper and print the picture to conform to the dimension 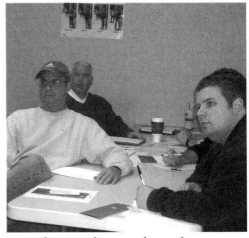 requirements above. Also, make sure that you have a plain white background behind you. Find a place in your house or garage that has a plain white wall behind you. It will not help your application if there is dark paneling and a 1939 church directory picture of your great aunt and uncle in the background.

You can also go to a store or shop that provides instant passport photos. The cost for instant passport photos is usually about $7.00 or $8.00 and you are virtually guaranteed that the agency will accept the photos. The store will usually provide a protective encasement also. However, make sure that you verify with the photographer that your full face will fall within the picture and that the picture will be in color. As a general rule, make sure that the photograph has been taken within about six months of the application date. Your goal here is to give the agency an accurate current photo so that the SLED clerk can match your application picture with your digitally recorded South Carolina Driver' License or ID on file (if you are a South Carolina resident).

Proof of Adequate Vision

You must also present proof that you have at least 20/40 vision. This can be natural 20/40 or it can be with glasses, contacts, or surgery, or whatever. If you are a South Carolina resident, your valid South Carolina driver's license satisfies this requirement. If you have one, you will not need any additional proof.

Proof of Firearms Training

You must also submit proof of training. This means that you must provide an original or a certified copy of a document that certifies that you have fulfilled one of the six statutory alternatives for training.

Basic Training Provided by CWP Class

If you have not completed one of the other proof of training alternatives, the best way to fulfill this requirement is to simply take a concealed weapons class from a SLED approved instructor. A list of SLED approved instructors can be found on GrassRoots' website www.SCFirearms.org under the "Training Information" button. By gaining your training this way, you know that you have fulfilled the statutory requirements for training. It should be noted though, that any SLED approved basic or advanced handgun education course offered by a state, county, or municipal law enforcement agency or a nationally recognized organization can potentially fulfill the training requirement if the required level of South Carolina statutory and case law is included.

For a course to fulfill the statutory requirements and be SLED approved, it must be a minimum of eight hours and it must include all of the following:

- Information on the statutory and case law of South Carolina;

- Information relating to handguns and on the use of deadly force;

- Information on handgun use and safety;

- Information on the proper storage practice for handguns (specifically with an emphasis on storage practices which reduce the possibility of accidental injury to children); and,

- The actual firing of the handgun in the presence of the instructor.

The eight-hour course (usually completed the same day) must include both a SLED approved written test and a firing range test after that day's instruction. The applicant must achieve at least a minimum score of seventy (70%) percent correct on the written test and a minimum score of seventy (70%) percent on the firing range qualification.

All of the topics in the written test will have been covered by the instructor in the course so you need not worry that you will be asked about topics that you have not been exposed to. A good instructor will make every effort to insure that his students are well prepared for the written test.

The range test determines if you are minimally competent with the handgun that you test with that day. Most instructors allow you to bring your own handgun. If you don't have one, they will generally provide a handgun for you. Do not go to the course without being sure that you either have your own functioning defensive handgun or that the instructor will have one that you can use that day.

On the day of the course, you will be required to shoot at a target from various distances. You will shoot at a large human-size silhouette target starting from 3 and then back to 15 yards, firing a total of 50 rounds. If you don't feel confident that you can get 35 of your 50 rounds into such a target, practice at the gun range before taking the course. Safety is paramount during the range test. As with the written portion of the test, good instructors are concerned that their students have every opportunity to pass the shooting portion of the class.

You must have completed the course within the three years prior to your application. Please save yourself grief and use a reputable trainer. Get assurance from the school that your training meets the requirements for a South Carolina Concealed Weapons Permit. Also, it might seem like a silly question to ask of the instructor, but make sure to verify that you will receive written evidence of completion of the training. It would be a shame to pay good money and go through training only to be snookered by someone who cannot provide the right training or proof of training. Best advice, use GrassRoots' list.

Alternative Proof of Training

There are five other ways to fulfill the statutory proof of training requirement. If you are a certified firearms instructor, you might not need any further training. To qualify for this alternative, you must be certified as an instructor by the NRA or other SLED approved national organization that promotes the safe use of handguns. You will have to contact SLED directly for a current list of approved organizations.

Second, you satisfy the training requirement if you can demonstrate to the director of SLED that you have a proficiency in the use of handguns and a thorough knowledge of South Carolina law pertaining to handguns. This method seems very uncommon and mysterious. If you want to try to satisfy the training requirement this way, you will have to contact SLED and petition to see if the administrator will accept the proof of that training that you are offering. Approval under this alternative is done on a case-by-case basis. Unless you have some extraordinary training and experience, you are advised to simply take an approved course.

A third alternative is for SLED certified or approved competitive handgun shooters. These designations are sanctioned and awarded by governing bodies like the United States Practical Shooting Association (USPSA), the International Defensive Pistol Association (IDPA), and the National Rifle Association (NRA). You must contact SLED directly to see if your handgun classification qualifies you for the proof of training required by the statute.

A fourth alternative is an active duty police handgun instructor. This category does not need any further explanation. You know if you are an active duty police handgun instructor.

Finally, certain military experience can provide proof of training under the statute. In general, you can submit proof that you are an active or reserve member of the military (including National Guard) and have had official military handgun training from your branch of service (Coast Guard, Air Force, Army, Marines, Navy) within the three years preceding the application. Once again, it's probably worthwhile to call SLED prior to applying to see if your military training qualifies for the exception.

A word of caution about the five alternatives to the basic training provided in concealed weapons classes from SLED approved trainers. Submitting proof of training through the alternatives does not necessarily expose you to the laws of self-defense, concealed weapons, firearms, etc. Therefore, you are encouraged to make sure that you are knowledgeable about South Carolina gun law. This book is a great tool but the authors also encourage you to consider taking the basic training that comes with a concealed weapons class.

Fingerprints

You must submit two complete original sets of fingerprints. You can get your fingerprints taken at any law enforcement agency or any other SLED approved fingerprint technician. A non-law enforcement trainer can be a SLED approved fingerprint technician.

The South Carolina Code of Laws provides that a law enforcement agency cannot charge you more than $5 for fingerprints associated with an application for a concealed weapons permit (South Carolina Code of Laws Section 23-31-215(A)(7)). If the officer demands more, the statutes do not authorize or support him. If you give the officer more, you could be contributing to his unofficial "lunch fund."

It is important that you use the fingerprint cards that SLED provides. To get your cards, call SLED at: (803) 896-7014. Note that this is a different number from other SLED numbers. Again, make sure that you get at least two cards because you will need to submit two original fingerprint cards with your application.

If you never had your fingerprints taken, it is simple. Appendix III discusses the process of getting your fingerprints in greater detail.

Exception to the Fingerprint Requirement

There is a very narrow exception to the fingerprint requirement contained in South Carolina Code of Laws Section 23-31-215(A)(7). The fingerprint requirement can be waived if you have a valid reason why it is impossible for you to produce a full set of fingerprints. Maybe you do not have ten fingers or you have a prosthetic or other condition. In this case, you must submit whatever fingerprints you can produce with a written statement from a licensed medical provider specifying the reason why a full set of your fingerprints cannot be taken.

Application Fee

In addition to the other requirements listed above, you will need to include the $50 application fee. This fee is waived if you are a disabled veteran or a retired law enforcement officer. From word of mouth, it seems that SLED will accept payment by personal check. Again though, as a general rule for payment to any government agency in any situation, your best bet is to send a money order or cashier's check. If you send a personal check, there is a chance that the agency will mail it back to you and make you start all over again.

The Role of SLED in Approval or Denial

Once you submit your application, SLED will begin conducting a multi-jurisdictional fingerprint review. They will also verify your claim of residency or qualified non-residency through local sheriffs. Furthermore, a criminal background check is performed. The sheriff of your county of residence will have ten working days to check your background and submit a recommendation to SLED. If the sheriff fails to complete the background check within ten working days, you get a favorable recommendation by default.

If all reviews performed and the sheriff's recommendation is favorable, SLED must issue the permit. If SLED denies your application, they must give you a written statement within 90 days from the date of the application specifying the reason for the denial. If they fail to give you the written denial within the 90 days, SLED must issue the permit by default.

If they do deny you your permit, you can appeal the decision. You have 30 days from the date you receive the denial notice to file a written appeal specifying the basis for your appeal. This appeal is submitted to the chief of SLED (the denial will give you who and where to send the appeal). SLED will then have 10 days from receiving your written appeal to issue a written decision. This written decision will either reverse the denial (granting you a permit) or uphold the denial. If the decision is to uphold the denial, SLED must specify the reasons why your denial is being upheld.

If your appeal results in SLED standing by its original denial, you then have the option of petitioning for review by an administrative law judge (ALJ). You must file your petition for ALJ review within 30 days of receiving your SLED appeal results. We will not get too in depth with the intricacies of administrative law here (the procedures are set out in South Carolina Code of Laws 1-23-380.) However, you should know that an appeal to an ALJ is limited in its scope. Basically, the administrative law judge can review only the record before him or her. The judge cannot substitute his or her own judgment for SLED's with respect to the weight of evidence or questions of fact. Even if the judge would have decided the case in your favor, he is required to uphold SLED's decision unless one of the following listed causes for *reversal* are involved. The judge may affirm SLED's decision or send your application back to SLED for further proceedings. Further, the judge may reverse or modify SLED's decision in narrow circumstances where substantial rights have been prejudiced because SLED's findings, inferences, conclusions, or decisions are:

- in violation of constitutional or statutory provisions;

- in excess of the statutory authority of the agency;

- made upon unlawful procedure;

- affected by other error of law;

- clearly erroneous in view of the reliable, probative, and substantial evidence on the whole record; or

- arbitrary or capricious or characterized by abuse of discretion or clearly unwarranted exercise of discretion.

If you want to appeal at this level, the administrative courts allow for you to represent yourself. You can save attorney's fees by organizing your appeal and presenting your case yourself. The administrative courts are generally held in a smaller courtroom with only the judge, the judge's assistant and the parties (with their attorneys if represented), and security. The rules of procedure and evidence are a little more relaxed than in a civil court of law.

The risk of representing yourself on your appeal is that you might not present your best case to the court. However, many people can organize and present their case very well without an attorney present at the hearing. Each individual appellant must make a cost/benefit analysis when deciding whether or not to hire an attorney for the appeal. If you are unsuccessful with your appeal, you can reapply for your CWP and start the process all over again. As a final note, if you want legal help, you should talk with an administrative law attorney or gun rights attorney WELL BEFORE your 30 day appeal window closes.

Once You Get Your Permit

Your permit will be valid statewide until it is revoked or expires. It will be revoked if you become prohibited from possessing a weapon, move to another state or no longer own property in the state (in the case of a qualified non-resident permit). If you get charged with a crime (that will makes it illegal for you to possess a firearm), and the permit will be revoked. However, if your permit is revoked because you got charged with a crime that will make it illegal for you to possess a firearm, and you are later found not guilty, your permit must be reinstated at no charge. If revoked, it must be surrendered to a sheriff, police department, or SLED agent. Alternatively, it can be sent by certified mail to the chief of SLED. If you fail to surrender the permit for the above reasons, you have committed a misdemeanor. If your permit is revoked because you have become a person prohibited under state law from possessing a weapon, your name, address, and reason for revocation will be published in an annual report by SLED (S.C. Code 23-31-215(T)(7)).

What if I am Approached by a Law Enforcement Officer?

At first glance, South Carolina Code 23-31-215(K) appears to provide that you must carry your permit card with you whenever you carry a concealable weapon, concealed. Additionally, it appears to require that if you have a concealable weapon, concealed, and a police officer identifies himself as a police officer and then asks for your identification or driver's license, you must inform the officer that you have a permit and present the permit to the officer. Failure to comply with this section is a misdemeanor. However, there is an important distinction that you must make with respect to this section. The next section explains this distinction.

The CWP Statute vs. Carrying Under an Exception

The statutory provision above is qualified with the words: [w]hen carrying a concealable weapon *pursuant to* [the concealed weapons permit statute]. So, what about if you are carrying a concealable weapon, concealed, **not** *pursuant to* the concealed weapons permit statute? In other words, what if you are legally carrying a concealable weapon under one of the handgun exceptions? For instance, there is a handgun exception allowing a handgun in your car glove box. The answer can only be found by conceptualizing two different ways to legally carry a concealable weapon.

You will learn in the next chapter that the general rule is that it is illegal to carry a handgun openly or concealed. There are however, exceptions to that general rule that permit you to legally carry a handgun. One is with the concealed weapons permit and the other is under one of the statutory exceptions (explained in the next chapter). If you want to legally carry a handgun, you must determine for yourself, "Am I carrying legally under the CWP statute or, alternatively, am I carrying legally under another statutory exception?"

Carrying Under the CWP Statute

This chapter primarily explains how and where you can carry if you have a concealed weapons permit.

Carrying Under a Statutory Exception

Another way to legally carry a handgun is under one of the other statutory exceptions. So, a person without a CWP can carry a handgun if they do so under an exception. The important point here though, is that even if you **do** have a CWP, you can none-the-less carry under one of the statutory exceptions.

Now, let's look at an example of how these two handgun carry concepts work with each other in the context of a vehicle. Say, for instance, that you are speeding in your car in South Carolina. Say also that you have a CWP and you are carrying a handgun in your front pocket that meets the definition of a concealable weapon. You also have your CWP (card) with you. At that point, you are legally carrying a handgun under the CWP statute.

You look in the rear view mirror and there is a police car with flashing lights behind you. You pull over and the police officer asks you for identification. Because you are carrying the handgun pursuant to the CWP statute, you are required to inform the officer that you have a concealed weapons permit.

Alternatively, what if all of the facts are the same except that the handgun has been in the glove compartment the entire time? One exception to the general prohibition on handguns allows handguns to be carried in the glove compartment of vehicles. Therefore, in this example, you are carrying pursuant to the statutory glove compartment exception and not pursuant to the CWP statute. Remember that the requirement to inform an officer exists only if carrying pursuant to the CWP statute. Following, there is no requirement that you VOLUNTEER to inform the officer that you have a CWP or that there is a handgun in the glove compartment. If the officer happens to ask if you have weapons in the car, you should tell the officer that you have a handgun in the glove box.

You can envision other instances where you must conceptualize whether you are carrying under a CWP or a statutory handgun exception. For instance, there is a statutory exception that permits licensed hunters and fishermen to carry a concealed handgun when hunting or fishing (discussed later in the book). If a person is a licensed fisherman and carrying a concealed handgun while fishing, he does not have to show a law enforcement officer his CWP permit card if asked for identification. Why not? He is carrying under a statutory exception and not under the CWP statute.

What if I have a Concealed Weapon when my Buddy is Pulled Over?

What do you do if you are a passenger in a car and the driver gets stopped by a police officer? If you are carrying a concealable weapon, concealed, under the CWP statute, you are only required to inform the officer that you have a CWP if the officer asks **you** for your identification. If the officer asks only the driver for his identification, other passengers are not required to volunteer that they have a CWP or that they have a concealed weapon. However, if the officer then turns to you and asks you for identification, you are required at that point to disclose that you have a CWP. If all handguns are in the glove box or otherwise carried under another statutory exception, nobody has to volunteer to the officer that they have a CWP when asked for identification.

The Practical Elements of a Law Enforcement Officer Road Stop

If ever stopped by a law enforcement officer while in your car, sit in your seat and keep your hands on the steering wheel. In most cases, the officer will approach you. Never make a move to get out of the car or reach for anything in the car. Simply sit in your seat with your hands on the wheel or otherwise in plain view. The first thing that the officer should do is identify him or herself. If the officer does not ask for driver's license or other identification, you do not have to volunteer that you have a concealed weapons permit. However, the officer is likely to ask for your driver's license, vehicle registration and proof of insurance. At that point, if you are carrying a concealable weapon, concealed, pursuant to the CWP Statute, inform the officer that you have a concealed weapons permit. The officer might then ask where the weapon is located. Inform the officer where the weapon is located but do not reach for it. The officer should then instruct you as to retrieving your license and paperwork.

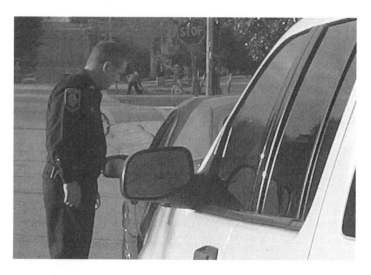

Alternatively, if you have your CWP but are legally carrying a handgun in the glove box (or other legal place) pursuant to the statutory exceptions, you do not have to volunteer to the officer that you have a CWP or that there is a handgun in the conveyance. But, what if the officer asks for registration paperwork and the paperwork is in the glove box or wherever the handgun is? Should you open the glove box and reach for the registration without first telling the officer that you have a handgun in the glove box? While there is no statutory provision requiring you to volunteer that you have a handgun in the glove box, not informing the officer could result in the officer drawing his weapon on you out of safety for his own self. So, you should inform the officer that you have the firearm in the glove box.

The main point is that you might not be required to produce your CWP or volunteer that you have a handgun if you fall under one of the other handgun exceptions. However, you must weigh that right against the possibility of causing the officer to draw his weapon out of a perceived need for self-defense. Also, there is always the possibility that an officer does not fully understand the law and might arrest you even though you were carrying legally under a statutory exception. Police are people too and they make mistakes. It is up to you to balance your rights against the practicalities of a police stop.

CWP vs. Exception Flow-Chart

Following is a CWP vs. exception flow-chart that helps organize the differences between carrying a concealed weapon, concealed under the CWP statute versus carrying a handgun under another statutory handgun exception. This chart is limited to a typical carry situation from your dwelling property, into your vehicle, and possibly getting pulled over by a law enforcement officer for speeding. (Carrying out of your car to work is discussed later in the book). The chart assumes that you are not legally disqualified from owning or possessing a firearm and that you are not fleeing after committing a crime.

Do you have a South Carolina Concealed
Weapons Permit (CWP)?
(or Reciprocity)

YES
You can choose to carry under the CWP
Statute <u>OR</u> a another statutory handgun
exception.

NO
You can **ONLY** carry a handgun under a
handgun exception.

You can have and carry any legal handgun -
concealed or openly - in your home or on your
private property.
See Sections 16-23-20(8) and (12).

You can have and carry any legal handgun -
concealed or openly - in your home or on your
private property. See Section 16-23-20(8).

You can carry a concealable weapon,
concealed, from your dwelling place to your
conveyance (vehicle) and make a diversion to
the mailbox, etc. You **MUST** have your CWP
card with you.
See Section 16-23-20(12).

OR ↓

You can carry any legal handgun, openly or
concealed, directly from your dwelling place to
your vehicle (including motorcycles) under 16-
23-20(15).

Once in your conveyance (vehicle), you can
carry the concealable weapon, concealed, on or
about your person (i.e. in your clothing, purse,
briefcase or work/computer bag).
See Section 16-23-20(9)(b).

OR ↓

Once in your vehicle, handguns **MUST** be
stored in a closed glove box, closed console or
in a secured container in the luggage
compartment of the vehicle under 16-23-
20(9)(a). (Saddlebags for motorcycles).
Exception for hunting, fishing or target/shows
under 16-23-20(3), (4), and (7).

If stopped by a law enforcement officer and
an officer asks <u>YOU</u> for identification, you
MUST show the officer your CWP card. If
YOU are in the conveyance and not asked
for YOUR ID, you do not have to show your
CWP. (**ONLY** the person asked by a law
enforcement officer for ID must produce his
or her CWP card.) Also, there
is no statutory requirement for anyone to
volunteer to the officer that there is a
firearm in the vehicle.

OR ↓

If you have a CWP but choose to carry under
the 16-23-20(9)(a) or (16) handgun exception
(i.e. handgun is in the glove box, console,
saddle bags or in a secured encasement in the
luggage compartment), you **DO NOT** have to
show the officer your CWP card. Also, there is
no statutory requirement for anyone to
volunteer to the officer that there is a firearm
in the vehicle.

Carrying without having the CWP Card with You

What if you are carrying a concealable weapon, concealed and you have a CWP, but you do not have the CWP identification card with you? Your CWP can be verified through the SLED computer over the dispatch. But even if the officer verifies that you have one, you are still in violation. You can be arrested and charged. In practice, the officer can let you go after him being satisfied of verification through dispatch over the radio. But you should never take that risk. It is the law that you always carry the CWP card with you whenever you have a concealable weapon, concealed with you.

Be aware that Section 16-23-460 (not even in the CWP Statute!) creates an additional penalty for carrying a concealed weapon not in compliance with the CWP Statute. The additional penalty is that your weapon must be forfeited and you either pay up to a $500 fine or serve 90 days in jail.

What if an Officer Wants Me to Get Out of the Car to Check Me for Weapons?

At any time, and even with no particular suspicion, an officer can pat you down to check for weapons. An officer always has a right to look after his or her own safety by briefly detaining you to pat you down for weapons. The officer can even handcuff you briefly while he or she pats you down. Just because you are being patted down or briefly handcuffed while the officer checks you does not mean that you are under arrest. If you are being placed under arrest, the office will inform you that you are being placed under arrest and read you a *Miranda* warning. If you are placed under arrest, you have a right to remain silent and you should always exercise that right and immediately ask for an attorney.

53

What if a Police Officer wants to Search my Car?

An officer has a right to search your car if he or she has **reasonable suspicion** that you or your passengers have been involved in criminal activity. The officer can search not only your car but also your person and objects belonging to you or any passengers. If an officer has a reasonable suspicion that you or your passengers have been involved in criminal activity, you are subject to search whether you have given permission or not. However, if the officer does not have reasonable suspicion, he or she cannot make a search without your permission. Whether or not the officer had a reasonable suspicion is ultimately up to a judge and not you.

Following are examples of where an officer probably has or probably does not have reasonable suspicion:

- Reasonable suspicion – The police get a call that somebody has pulled a gun at someone's house. The person who pulled the gun is described as a white male with blue ball cap driving a big green car. You are stopped for speeding several blocks from the home where the gun was brandished. You are a white male and you drive a green four door car. Many people might fit the description of a white male with a big green car but, additionally, the fact that you were also speeding close to the scene raises a reasonable suspicion.

- No reasonable suspicion – You are a white male with a big green car. The police have no reports of crime in the area. You run a stop sign. The officer has no reasonable suspicion that you are involved in criminal activity just because you ran a stop sign.

What if you are not in a car but rather stopped on the street while carrying a concealable weapon, concealed with a CWP? If you are approached by an officer on the street, you have no legal duty to inform the officer that you have a CWP or a weapon unless the officer asks you for identification. If the officer does ask you for ID, immediately inform the officer that you have a permit. As a practical matter, tell the officer exactly where the CWP and weapon is located. Don't reach or grab for your permit or the weapon. Resist the tendency to touch your weapon because people have a natural tendency to touch a weapon when they are indicating its location. Keep your hands away from your weapon and simply tell the officer where the weapon is located.

Again, the officer is allowed to pat you down for safety. Similarly, the officer can search you and your belongings if he or she has a reasonable suspicion that you have been involved in criminal activity. However, if the officer has no reasonable suspicion, he or she can only search with your permission.

In summary, a law enforcement officer can search you, your vehicle and your belongings without your permission if the officer has reasonable suspicion that you have been involved in criminal activity. If the officer has no reasonable suspicion, the officer can only search with your permission or any evidence obtained is vulnerable to being suppressed in court. If you give permission for a search, any evidence found is admissible in court even if it would not have been admissible if your permission had not been granted.

So, in a practical sense, you should never give a law enforcement officer permission for a search. If the law enforcement officer had probable cause, he would not be asking for permission. If the law enforcement officer does not have probable cause, do not give him access for a search.

We use the term reasonable suspicion synonymously with probable cause. Do not get hung up between these two terms because, for all intents and purposes, they men the same thing. Theoretically, probable cause is supposed to be a higher standard than reasonable suspicion. In reality though, Courts find it very difficult to define a difference between the two. A detailed analysis of a supposed difference in these terms is beyond the scope of this book and easily convoluted enough to take-up volumes of law books. The bottom line is that a Court will decide if the law enforcement officer had sufficient reasonable suspicion or probable cause to conduct and search or make an arrest.

Law Enforcement Officers can be Wrong

The authors of this book have the utmost respect for law enforcement officers. In fact, one of the authors is a law enforcement officer. Law enforcement officers go through tremendous training and continuing education. Like the rest of us, however, they are not perfect and they can make mistakes.

Even though you might be legally correct in a situation involving firearms, there is plenty of room for error on the part of the officer. You might still be stopped, interrogated, searched, harassed or even arrested for carrying a firearm or other dangerous weapon. Legal questions can be left to a judge to sort out. So, get your CWP and follow the law but also be aware that having a CWP and following the law is not an absolute guarantee against a misunderstanding that results in embarrassment, discomfort, or an expensive legal headache.

Unlawful Places to Carry Even with a Concealed Weapons Permit

Even with a permit, the South Carolina Code of Laws makes it a crime to willfully carry a handgun into certain places. Do not knowingly bring a handgun into:

- A business that sells alcoholic beverages for onsite consumption (unless you are an owner or person in legal control of that business as discussed later in this chapter);

- A police, sheriff, or highway patrol station, or any other law enforcement office or facility;

- A detention facility, prison, jail, or other correctional facility or Office;

- A courthouse or courtroom;

- A polling place on an election day;

- The office of, or the business meeting of, the governing body of a county, public school district, municipality, or special purpose district;

- Any school (without the express permission from school authorities), see *The Rules for Schools* in the chapter on *Possessing and Transporting a Gun without a Permit* for a more thorough discussion of weapons on school grounds or activities;

- A daycare facility or pre-school facility (without permission);

- A place where the carrying of a firearm is prohibited by Federal Law like federal buildings, federal lands, military bases, (without permission);

- A church or other established religious sanctuary unless you have express permission of the appropriate church official or governing body; or,

- A hospital, medical clinic, doctor's office, or any other facility where medical procedures are performed unless you are authorized by the employer.

Even with a CWP, if you willfully carry into one of these places you can be charged with a misdemeanor and the punishment is a fine of at least $1,000 or a jail sentence of up to one year, or both, in the discretion of the court (South Carolina Code of Laws Section 23-31-215(M). You will also have your permit revoked for 5 years.

If you bring your handgun into a business that sells alcoholic beverages for onsite consumption the crime is a also a misdemeanor but the possible penalty is a fine of not more than $2,000 or jail for not more than three years or both (South Carolina Code of Laws Section 16-23-465). Also, if you were carrying under your CWP the permit will be revoked (the statute does not say for how long). This crime and penalty does not apply if you are the owner or person in legal control of the business. The rules for business owners or those in legal control are discussed in another section of this book.

The potential 3 year jail term for the offense discussed above is longer than the typical penalty for misdemeanors (not more than 1 year in jail). However, not only is the potential penalty more than those other misdemeanors, it significantly differs because it places the convicted offender into federal firearms disability territory. Federal firearms disability arises when a person is convicted of a federal crime that carries the *potential* penalty of more than one (1) year in jail or a state felony, or a state misdemeanor that carries a *potential* penalty of greater than 2 years in jail. Even though carrying into a business that sells alcohol for onsite consumption is a misdemeanor, the potential penalty is three years in jail. So, even if you were to "plea down" to six months in jail, the fact that the potential penalty is up to 3 years sticks you with a federal firearms disability.

There is more bad news. All of the offenses in this section of this chapter of the book are subject to the additional penalties created in South Carolina Code of Laws Section 16-23-460. These penalties arise if convicted of carrying a concealed weapon not in compliance with the CWP Statute. The additional penalty is that your weapon must be forfeited and you either pay up to a $500 fine or serve 90 days in jail.

Special Permission

You can get special permission to possess firearms from authorized individuals at places like schools, hospitals, doctor's offices, and churches. However, you must get the express permission of the presiding officer of the institution to be exempted. Express permission means a positive offer and acceptance of permission. As a rule of thumb, you will want this permission in writing on the official letterhead of the institution. Make sure the permission is from the presiding officer or presiding body. Examples would be the university president and university chief of police, hospital physical plant chief, doctor who owns the medical clinic, or church pastor, deaconate or presbytery.

Also, not withstanding the list, it appears that you can get a form of "special permission" to carry concealable weapons and other handguns onto and into places like military bases and state and local government buildings. Getting "special permission" from the person in charge of the institution is not a part of the concealed weapons permit statute but, instead, seems to have informally evolved from the college handgun exception found in Section 16-23-420 and the exceptions in the preceding paragraph that arise from the concealed weapons permit statute.

Where does this exception come into play? Sometimes you will see gun shows in public buildings or county fairgrounds facilities. Also, some military bases sponsor shooting competitions. Beyond these events, there might be instances where the city building official or base commander thinks it appropriate to allow certain individuals the ability to have concealable weapons or other weapons on the premises. The simple rule is to always get written permission from the presiding official on the letterhead of the institution. If you feel comfortable with, or can only get verbal permission, that is your call. Just remember to make absolutely certain that you have official permission and that the person who gave you permission will back you up in court if it comes to that. If not, you are risking serious consequences to your ability to lawfully possess and carry a gun.

Take special note that there are virtually no instances where non-law enforcement officials are allowed to carry handguns (or any firearms) into courthouses. South Carolina law prohibits firearms in courthouses and federal law prohibits firearms in federal courthouses. 18 U.S.C. 930(g)(3) defines a "Federal Court Facility" as the courtroom, judges' chambers, witness rooms, jury deliberation rooms, attorney conference rooms, prisoner holding cells, offices of the court clerks, the United States attorney, and the United States marshal, probation and parole offices, and adjoining corridors of any court of the United States.

Special Privileges for Some Permit Holders

Certain people can carry their concealable weapons, concealed, anywhere in the state as long as they have a concealed weapons permit and are carrying out the duties of their office. Privilege holders include:

- most judges;

- prosecutors and assistant prosecutors; and

- worker's compensation commissioners.

If you are one of these folks and have a permit, you can carry a concealable weapon into courthouses or wherever else your official duties take you.

There are two issues involved in analyzing this provision. The first is whether or not you are one of these special people. If you are one of these people, you know it. The second issue is whether or not you are carrying out the duties of your office. It is pretty clear that a judge sitting on his or her bench during a trial is carrying out official duties. Likewise, an assistant prosecutor interviewing a witness in a government building is carrying out his or her official duties. (Prosecutors must follow individual jail, prison or other incarceration facility rules though).

Say, though, that a worker's compensation commissioner is investigating a case and is required to talk with someone in a business that serves alcoholic beverages? That would seem to fall under official duties and the commissioner's carry is legal. Likewise, what if a prosecutor is investigating the facts of a case and is required to inspect areas of a school? That too would seem to fall under the exception and the concealed carry would be legal. A search for case law on this issue turned up nothing, probably because the type of people who are the subject of this provision do not get arrested for carrying concealed weapons very often. If this provision applies to you, you likely have legal education and experience. Therefore, all we can say is use your best judgment in determining the extent of this provision.

Can I Carry into a U.S. Post Office?

With or without a CWP, you are prohibited from bringing a handgun into a U.S. Post Office under South Carolina Code of Laws Section 16-23-420. That statue makes it a crime to carry a handgun into a publicly owned building. The crime is a felony that carries a prison term not to exceed five (5) years and a fine of no more than $5,000 or both. Conviction on the charge also burdens you with a lifetime federal firearms disability. Don't forget the additional penalties of Section 16-23-460 (weapon must be forfeited and you either pay up to a $500 fine or serve 90 days in jail).

Retail Mail Stores

An alternative to U.S. Post Offices is retail mailing stores that sell stamps, packaging materials, mailbox services, and shipping services. Typically these stores are located in shopping centers, malls, or in stand alone buildings. These stores are generally classified as *contract post offices* under 39 Code of Federal Regulations 241.2. Because they are wholly private, they are not considered federal property and you are not prevented from carrying a concealable weapon, concealed into those stores.

Carrying at a Bank or ATM Machine

Because banks are highly regulated by the federal government, many people confuse banks for federal property. Banks are private companies that are insured and heavily watched by the federal government but are not owned by the federal government (at least not yet) and are not federal property. You are not prohibited from carrying a concealable weapon, concealed, into a bank if you have your permit. Be on the lookout, however, for banks that post a statutorily compliant "No Concealable Weapons" sign discussed later in this chapter. If that sign is up and it conforms to the statute, you cannot bring your concealable weapon, concealed into the building. You can still use the outside ATM and not break any law though.

Credit Unions

Many credit unions have the term "Federal Credit Union" in the name or on the paperwork. Like banks, credit unions are regulated by the federal government but are not the property of the United States government. The same rules that apply for banks apply to federal credit unions.

Businesses that Serve Alcohol on the Premises

If you are carrying a concealable weapon, concealed, you must be careful not to enter a business that sells alcoholic liquors, beers or wines for on-premises consumption. For business owners, employees and those in legal control of a business, this topic is explored in greater detail later in this chapter and in the chapter on possessing and transporting handguns without a concealed weapons permit.

As a patron of a particular business, you might say, "Hold on! My favorite restaurant serves beer and wine. Can I carry my concealed weapon into the restaurant if I have my permit?" The answer is no. In 2001, then SLED chief Robert Stewart asked for an attorney general's opinion on this issue. The *informal* (not formal) opinion for the South Carolina Attorney General was written by assistant attorney general David K. Avant. The official opinion concludes:

> As the law of this State is currently written, a concealed weapons permit holder may not carry a firearm onto the premises of an establishment which serves alcohol. Any establishment which serves alcohol on the premises is included in the prohibition – bar and restaurant alike.

(A formal attorney general (AG) opinion may be issued by the Attorney General in response to requests by state agency officials to help them perform their duties. These opinions are not law, but advice to state officials on questions of law and how the law applies to particular fact situations. So, while not carrying the full force and effect of law, an AG opinion is none-the-less persuasive and often relied upon by government officials as if the opinion was law. An informal AG opinion carries less weight.)

Based upon South Carolina Code of Laws Section16-23-465 and the AG opinion, you should assume that law enforcement officers will arrest and charge anyone carrying a pistol or firearm into a business that sells alcoholic beverages for on-site consumption. A violation of this section brings a penalty including a fine not more than $2,000 or imprisonment for not more than 3 years, or both. You will also get your permit revoked. Again, because the potential penalty of this state misdemeanor is greater than 2 years in jail, a conviction under this statute subjects you to a lifetime Federal firearms disability. This law needs to be changed to allow CWP holders to enter these businesses without fear of a criminal charge. Contact your representatives and demand that CWP holders be allowed to carry into businesses that sell alcohol for onsite consumption.

Remember that this prohibition is against carrying a pistol or other firearm into a business that sells alcohol for on-premises consumption. It does not prohibit you from carrying another type of weapon or up to 50cc of pepper spray concealed (*see also* South Carolina Code of Laws Section 23-31-215(O)(2)). Neither does it prevent you from carrying a concealable weapon, concealed into a package liquor store, convenience store or bulk store if alcohol is not served for on-site consumption in that business.

Sometimes, upscale groceries stores will have wine sampling. Technically this would trigger the prohibition if the store is selling the samples for onsite consumption. However, if the store is giving the samples with the hope that you will purchase a bottle to take out of the store to drink, the statute is not violated. Regardless of whether a business technically serves alcohol or not though, always be on the lookout for a "NO CONCELABLE WEAPONS ALLOWED" sign on the storefront. We will talk about that sign next.

Businesses that Do Not Want You to Carry in Their Building

Even though the state provides for the issuance of concealed weapons permits, it also protects the rights of employers and property owners. An employer may prohibit a permit holder from carrying a concealed weapon on the business property. It further allows the business owner to prohibit employees from carrying concealed weapons at off-site work places or while using any machinery, vehicles, or equipment owned or operated by the business. In a nutshell, a business can prohibit permit carriers from carrying on the business premises or property like machinery or vehicles.

For example, say that you work as a repairman for a power company. Say also that the company chooses to prohibit guns at work under both the CWP Statute and also by a policy or condition of the workplace. The company provides you a vehicle and sends you to locations away from the office to repair power lines that the company owns. You are doing offsite repairs and driving a company vehicle to and from the offsite location. In this case, the employer can prevent you from carrying under your CWP the entire time that you are at work because the company owns or controls the office, the vehicle that you use to get to and from the offsite location, and the offsite location. Therefore, you can face both criminal liability under the CWP statute and private employment action by your employer if your employer for violating the policy or condition against carrying guns at work.

Next, let's look at a pizza delivery person using his personal vehicle to deliver pizzas for a company that chooses to disallow guns at work under both the CWP Statute and a policy or condition of the workplace. While picking up a pizza at the store, the driver would be prohibited by the *business property* language of the statute. While at the property of a customer, the driver would probably be prohibited by the *work place* language of the Statute. But, while driving his personally owned vehicle between the work place and the property of delivery, he would be free to carry pursuant to the CWP law even if he was on the clock. The way to accomplish this is to carry the handgun according to a handgun exception (i.e. glove box or console) while on work property and carry according to the CWP Statute (i.e. on, or about, the person) when inside the private vehicle. As in the previous example, the employer could still take employment action against him if it was discovered he had guns at work in violation of a company policy or condition. However, the employer could not invoke the police powers of the state to further punish the delivery person with a crime.

In addition to businesses, an owner or lawful tenant of private property can prohibit people from carrying concealed weapons upon the property. So even if the owner of the land is not your employer he can nonetheless prohibit you from carrying on his property. To legally prevent a permit holder from carrying on their property, the business, owner, or tenant must give proper notice. A sign that meets the statutory requirements for dimensions, etc. is constructive notice. But, actual notice is also allowed even if a sign is not posted. Thus, an employer can refuse to post a sign, thereby allowing the general public to legally carry with their CWP while also informing each employee that he can not carry. In so doing, the police powers of the state could not be used against a member of the general public but could be used against offending employees.

For constructive notice to anyone (general public or employee) that enters the property, the Code of Laws requires a sign that reads, "NO CONCEALABLE WEAPONS ALLOWED." The sign must be in both written language and in universal sign language. Braille is not required, presumably because all permit holders have met the SLED 20/40 vision requirement.

Required Sign

A conforming sign must be posted at each entrance where a concealed weapons permit holder might enter. It must be clearly visible from the outside of the building with a width of eight (8") inches and a height of twelve (12") inches. The words "NO CONCEALABLE WEAPONS ALLOWED" must be included, typeset in black, and one (1") inch tall. The letters must be all uppercase type and placed at the bottom of the sign and centered between the lateral edges of the sign.

Additionally, the sign must have a black silhouette of a handgun inside a circle which is seven (7") inches in diameter with a diagonal horizontal line that runs from the lower left to the upper right at a forty-five degree angle. The Code of Laws specify that the circle "must have a diameter of a circle." This seems to suggest that the circle must be a perfectly round circle and not a fancy oval or elliptical orbit shape. Finally, the sign must be placed not less than forty inches and not more than sixty inches from the bottom of the entrance door. If the place where concealed weapons are prohibited does not have doors, the signs must be bigger. To be specific, thirty-six (36") inches wide and forty-eight (48") inches tall. Again, it must contain the words "NO CONCEALABLE WEAPONS ALLOWED" in black three inch tall uppercase type at the bottom of the sign and centered between the lateral edges. It must have a black silhouette of a handgun inside a circle which is thirty-four (34") inches in diameter with a diagonal line that is two (2) inches wide and runs from the lower left to the upper right at a forty-five degree angle. The circle portion must be two inches wide just as the diagonal line is two inches wide. The sign must be placed not less that forty (40") inches and not more than ninety-six (96") inches above the ground. The purpose of these specifications is to standardize the signs. Therefore, a sign **must meet these specifications to be legal and enforceable against CWP permit holders**. The sign must also be posted in sufficient quantities to be clearly visible from any point of entry into the area where concealable weapons are prohibited.

Penalty for Carrying into a Prohibited Business

If you carry your concealed weapon inside in spite of the sign, you can be punished in accordance with Section 16-11-620. The charge is basically trespassing. You could be fined up to $200 or jailed for up to 30 days. Additionally, if you are charged a second or subsequent time, your permit will be revoked for one (1) year. These prohibitions do not apply to law enforcement officers. Again, don't forget the additional penalties of Section 16-23-460 (weapon must be forfeited and you either pay up to a $500 fine or serve 90 days in jail).

All that being said, why would you want to do business at a place that actively opposes your right to keep and bear arms anyway? Plus, criminals might target businesses where they think there is less of a chance to encounter armed resistance from a CWP carrier. Therefore, take your business elsewhere.

Lawsuit Protection for Business Owners

If you own a business which is open to the public, you might be thinking about the liability involved in having people coming into your business with concealed weapons. You might think that if you don't have a sign prohibiting people from carrying concealed weapons into your business, you will be opening yourself up to civil liability if a patron with a concealed weapon has to use it on a criminal. The legislature has anticipated scenarios where injured criminals or their families attempt to sue a business owner simply because the owner allowed the legally armed patron to carry concealed in his or her store. The South Carolina Code of Laws provides that businesses that allow their patrons to carry concealed weapons cannot be sued simply because the business allowed the armed patrons.

As a side note, business owners should be aware that they face potential liability for shootings on other legal theories and causes of action. Mainly, business and property owners face liability if they knew of a history or propensity for violent attacks on the premises and failed to protect patrons. For instance, a person shot in a store by an armed robber might argue that the business knew about prior attacks and did nothing to warn customers about the prior attacks. Similarly, a plaintiff could argue that the business failed to provide security or failed to provide enough light in the parking lot. Business owners should carefully follow all recommendations from their risk management office or liability insurance carrier regarding risk minimization and preventative best practices. Insurance companies are usually eager to give advice about risk management or to send out one of their agents to conduct a risk assessment. If your carrier does not gladly offer such a service, look for a better carrier.

It should also be noted that prohibiting or discouraging armed CWP holders on your property might create an attractive environment for criminals. If a business exercises the NO CONCEALED WEAPONS ALLOWED sign, a criminal might see that business as an attractive place to commit a crime. If a criminal or deranged gunman has a choice of operating in a gun free zone as opposed or one that welcomes CWP holders, logic says he will choose the gun free zone. Therefore, it could be argued that a business owner created an unsafe environment for the patrons of the business by posting such signs prohibiting CWP carry and the business should be held legally responsible for the additional danger created by the posting of the signs prohibiting CWP carry.

Business Owners, Managers and Employees

With or without a permit, a business owner, or the person in legal control of the business, may possess any legal firearm while on the premises of the business. The owner or person in legal control can carry a firearm either concealed or openly. This is true even if the business serves alcohol on the premises. Further, the owner or person in legal control of the business may grant permission to his employees to carry firearms openly or concealed while in the business (with the sole exception of businesses that sell alcoholic beer, wines, and liquors for on-site consumption).

In order for employees to carry while at work, they must determine whether they can legally carry pursuant to their concealed weapons permit or pursuant to an exception to the general statutory handgun prohibition. In other words, there are two ways for an employee to legally carry at work but the employee must make sure that he or she falls under one of the two statutorily created exceptions.

One way an employee can legally carry at work is by carrying under a concealed weapons permit pursuant to South Carolina Code of Laws Section 16-23-20(12). Under this provision of the concealed weapons permit law, an employee can carry a concealable weapon, concealed into his work without first obtaining his employer's permission (and even knowledge). However, the employee cannot carry pursuant to a concealed weapons permit if the business sells alcoholic beer, wine or liquors for on-site consumption. Likewise, an employee cannot carry under the concealed weapons permit statute if the employer has erected a proper NO CONCEALED WEAPONS ALLOWED sign on the premises.

Another way an employee can carry at work is under the South Carolina Code of Laws Section 16-23-20(13) exception. Under this exception, an employee can carry any legal firearm at work, open or concealed, so long as the employee has the permission of the owner or person in legal control *and* has a concealed weapons permit. Even under this permissive exception, though, employees of a business that sells alcohol for on-site consumption cannot carry a pistol or firearm while on the business premises. Note that, even though carrying at work under this exception requires an employee to have a CWP, the employee is not carrying pursuant to the permit but pursuant to the statutory exception. Therefore, the employee may carry openly and may carry firearms different from those defined previously in this chapter as "concealable weapons." Further, an employee carrying under this statutory exception may carry at a business that posts the NO CONCEALED WEAPONS ALLOWED sign because the employee has the business owner's (or the person in legal control's) permission.

It is important for an employee to recognize the difference between the legal and business policy rules for guns at work. The above two statutory exceptions are legal rules for carrying a firearm at work. An employee's failure to carry properly pursuant to one of those two exceptions exposes the employee to criminal arrest and prosecution. Alternatively, the employee should also determine if the company has a firearm policy that would prevent him or her from possessing guns at work. If the company has a policy against employees carrying guns at work, the employee could face discipline or be fired regardless of what the statutes say about employees carrying firearms at work.

Guns at Work Chart

	Owner	Person in Legal Control of Business	Employee
Do I need a CWP to carry any legal firearm at the business or store where I work (not including offsite work areas)?	No	No	**Yes,** whether carrying under S.C. Code 16-23-20(13) or carrying under 16-23-20(12).
Can I carry any sized firearm at a business or work?	Yes	Yes	**Yes,** if carrying under S.C. Code 16-23-20(13). Need Employer's Permission. **No,** if carrying under S.C. Code 16-23-20(12) can only carry a concealable weapon as defined by the CWP law.
Can I carry at a business or work that sells beer, wine or alcoholic liquors for on-site consumption?	Yes	Yes	No
Can I carry openly (i.e. on my hip) at a business or work?	Yes	Yes	**Yes,** can carry openly or concealed if carrying under S.C. Code 16-23-20(13) – read it though! **No,** can only carry concealable weapon, concealed, if carrying under 16-23-20(12).
Can I carry a handgun, openly or concealed, to and from the business and my vehicle under the Section 16-23-20(15) exception?	Yes	Yes	**Yes,** can carry openly or concealed under S.C. Code 16-23-20(15), directly to or from vehicle **IF** it is legal for you to have gun in the business.

Other People's Homes or Dwellings

Permit holders may not carry a concealable weapon, concealed, into the residence or dwelling of another person without the express consent of the owner or tenant. If you do, you can be charged with a misdemeanor and can be punished by a fine of not less than $1,000 or up to one year in jail or both. Also, your permit will be revoked for 5 years. Don't forget the additional penalties of Section 16-23-460 (weapon must be forfeited and you either pay up to a $500 fine or serve 90 days in jail). Do not go to someone else's place with a concealed weapon unless they give you their permission or you are absolutely sure that they do not have a problem with you carrying on their premises.

From Car to Home and Vice Versa with a Permit

With or without a CWP, you can carry a handgun, concealed or not, from your car to your house or apartment and from your house or apartment to your vehicle. If you do not have a CWP, you must go directly from your home to your vehicle or vice versa. Having the CWP additionally allows you to take a diversion to the mailbox, walk around the neighborhood, talk with the neighbors, etc. if your handgun is a concealable weapon, concealed. If you do not have a CWP, this provision is dealt with in more detail in the chapter on possessing and transporting handguns without a concealed weapons permit.

Partial Exception for CWP Holders on the Capitol Grounds

Section 10-11-320 of the South Carolina Code of Laws makes it unlawful to carry a firearm while on the capitol grounds or within the capitol building. The section defines capitol grounds as, "that area inward from the vehicular traveled surfaces of Gervais, Sumter, Senate and Assembly Streets in the city of Columbia."

There is somewhat of an exception for CWP holders though. Section 10-11-320(B) provides that a CWP holder who is authorized to park on the capitol grounds or in the parking garage below the capitol grounds may have a firearm in the vehicle. However, the firearm must remain locked in the CWP holder's vehicle while on or below the capitol grounds and must be stored in a place in the vehicle that is not readily accessible to any person upon that person's entry to or below the capitol grounds. The best practice here is to place the firearm in the trunk or luggage compartment of the vehicle before entering the capitol grounds and then return it to any other legal location on your person or in the vehicle after you leave the capitol grounds. See the *Can I Carry on the Capitol Grounds* section in the *Possessing and Transporting Guns without a Permit* chapter for more information about the prohibition and the penalties for violations.

Permit Reciprocity with Other States

If you have a valid permit from another state that has a reciprocal agreement with South Carolina, you can legally carry a concealed weapon just as if you have a South Carolina permit. Currently, only a handful of states have a reciprocity compact with South Carolina. The current states with South Carolina reciprocity are: Alaska, Arizona, Arkansas, Florida, Kansas, Kentucky, Louisiana, Michigan, Missouri, North Carolina, Ohio, Tennessee, Texas, Virginia, West Virginia and Wyoming. Check the SLED website periodically for the most current list of reciprocal states.

If you are in another state, and carry using the reciprocity or recognition function of your South Carolina CWP, you must be careful to follow the CWP rules for the state that you are in. In other words, if you have a South Carolina CWP, and are carrying in West Virginia, you need to know West Virginia CWP law. Generally, CWP laws are similar in most states but important distinctions do exist. For instance, in South Carolina, you can carry into banks that don't have a

"NO CONCLEABLE WEAPONS ALLOWED" sign. However, in North Carolina you are prohibited from carrying into any bank.

Carrying in North Carolina and Georgia

Because North Carolina and Georgia border South Carolina, you might need to know if and how you can carry in these states. This section is not comprehensive but gives a quick general guide. For complete information about carrying in these neighboring states, you will have to read the statutes and cases for a given state. We will start with North Carolina because it has a reciprocal agreement with South Carolina. If you have a South Carolina permit, you can carry a concealed handgun in North Carolina. You must always carry your permit with you and, if stopped by a law enforcement officer, you must indicate to the officer that you have a permit and indicate where the weapon is located. You should follow the same prohibitions as if you were in South Carolina with respect to government property, federal buildings and businesses that post a no weapons or firearms sign. Additionally, you cannot carry at schools, events that charge an admission fee like sports and theaters, and any place that sells alcoholic beverages. As in South Carolina, you specifically have the right to take your concealed weapon with you into highway rest area bathrooms. Different from South Carolina is that you cannot carry at financial institutions like banks. Different also is that you cannot carry at a parade, funeral procession, picket line or political protest. Apart from these differences, however, if you follow the South Carolina rules while in North Carolina, you should stay out of trouble.

Because Georgia does not have reciprocity with South Carolina, you have no special privileges with respect to carrying a concealable weapon. The general rules for transporting and possessing a weapon out of state are reviewed in the *Possessing and Transporting a Handgun without a Permit* chapter.

Be advised that there is a way to have a reciprocal concealed weapons permit for Georgia. As a South Carolina resident, you can obtain a New Hampshire Non-Resident Concealed Weapons Permit. New Hampshire has a reciprocity agreement with Georgia so New Hampshire permit holders can legally carry while in Georgia. For an application and more information, see the documents and forms page of the New Hampshire Department of Safety, Division of State Police at: http://www.nh.gov/safety/divisions/nhsp/forms.html.

Renewal of the South Carolina Concealed Weapons Permit

Your permit is good for four (4) years. You can renew the permit by completing SLED application Form R-078 (check the "Renewal" box instead of "New Application" box this time) and paying a $50 renewal fee. As with the original application, if you are a disabled veteran or a retired law enforcement officer, the $50 fee will be waived. If you let your previous permit expire for longer than sixty (60) days, SLED might require proof of new training. Finally, the checklist doesn't specify so but the statute requires that you also submit a photocopy of your valid South Carolina driver's license or identification card.

If you are a qualified non-resident, you've got a little more work on your hands. In addition to the application and fee, you must submit a photocopy of your valid driver's license or identification card from your state of residence. You must also send a new photo of your face. The photo can be no larger than 3" X 5". Just like when you originally applied, you must again submit a newly certified SLED Form R-168 (South Carolina Non-Resident Concealed Weapon Permit (CWP) Real Property Tax Form). This lets SLED know that you still own real estate in South Carolina.

Once you submit these things, SLED will again conduct a federal, state and local fingerprint review. If the background check is favorable, the permit will be renewed. SLED indicates that it will take about thirty (30) days to process your renewal.

Be mindful of your residency or qualified non-residency status. If you move to South Carolina, you are now a resident and should apply for a resident concealed weapons permit. If you retain an ownership interest in South Carolina real estate, you are still a qualified non-resident. If you sold your interest in South Carolina real estate, your permit became void at that point and you should have surrendered your qualified non-resident permit.

Lost or Stolen Permit

If your permit is lost or stolen, tell SLED immediately. Failure to tell them immediately is a misdemeanor with the penalty of a $25 fine. There's really no reason not to notify SLED considering that when you notify them, they will issue a replacement permit. Without the replacement permit, you won't be able to carry, so report it right away if you lose it. If you change your address, you must notify SLED in writing within 10 days. Along with your written notification, you must send $5. SLED will then issue a new permit that includes your new address. Generally, SLED has a very quick turn-around time for reissue after an address change. When you get the new permit, you must send the old permit back to SLED. If you are stopped and the officer discovers that the address on your permit is incorrect, you are subject to a misdemeanor with a fine of $25. The misdemeanor on your record stinks and so does a $25 fine but don't forget the additional penalties of Section 16-23-460 (weapon must be forfeited and you either pay up to a $500 fine or serve 90 days in jail). If you are abiding by the change of address law, however, and are doing so within the time limits set by that statute, you should not be subject to the original misdemeanor or the additional penalties of Section 16-23-460.

Permit Holder List is not Public Information

Can the public find out that you have a concealed weapons permit? For most folks, no. SLED maintains a list of all permit holders and the current status of each permit. In the spring of 2008, the South Carolina legislature passed H3528 which amended Section 23-31-215. The amended statute now requires SLED to keep the list free from public inquiry except under very limited circumstances. The practical effect of this legislation is to keep the identity of concealed weapons permit holders from the public eye. Be cautioned that permit holders who have their permit taken away as a result of a lifetime federal firearms disability or South Carolina Code of Laws Section 16-23-30(B) will be subject to public inquiry and disclosure.

Summary Points

- Go get your concealed weapons permit now if you are eligible to do so.

- Always have your permit with you if you are carrying a concealable weapon, concealed.

- Understand the difference between carrying under the concealed weapons permit statute or another statutory exception.

- Even with a permit, there are certain places you can't carry your concealed weapon, including *any* business that serves alcohol for onsite consumption unless you own the business or are in legal control of that business.

- With a concealed weapons permit, employees can carry concealable weapons, concealed while at work so long as the business owner or person in legal control does not give the employee notice not to carry a weapon and the business does not sell beer, wine or alcoholic liquors for on-site consumption.

- If you carry a firearm pursuant to the permit, make sure that your firearm meets the definition of a concealable weapon and that you carry it concealed at all times.

- With the permit, you can carry a concealable weapon, concealed onto State of South Carolina public interstate highway rest area property (including inside buildings and bathrooms).

- You have constitutional protections against both unreasonable searches and seizures and against compelled self-incrimination. Although a law enforcement officer may search anywhere within your reach (in plain view) without a search warrant after a valid stop, they may not search further in your vehicle nor open and search closed luggage without probable cause to believe evidence of a crime will be found, unless you consent. This is particularly true regarding locked storage areas or in the trunk of a vehicle.

- You may be required to produce a driver's license, vehicle registration, and, perhaps, proof of automobile insurance to a law enforcement officer, but you also have the right to remain silent.

Chapter 5
Possessing and Transporting Guns without a Permit

Whether you are a weekend shooter, gun collector, or have a weapon for self-defense, there is a good chance that you will transport or carry the weapon outside of your home. If you do not have a concealed weapons permit, it is essential that you know the rules for transporting or carrying a weapon without a permit. This chapter deals with possessing and transporting without a concealed weapons permit.

If you get any lesson from this chapter, it should be to always assess the legality of your gun's location. You should also see the value of getting a concealed weapons permit if you are eligible for one. The permit allows you to legally carry in many more situations than without one.

Handguns

So, where and when can you carry your gun? First let's start with the general rule. The general rule is that you cannot legally possess or carry a *handgun*, openly or concealed, unless you fall within a statutory exception to the general rule. Violation of this rule is a misdemeanor that carries a potential penalty of $1,000 and up to 1 year in jail under South Carolina Code of Laws Section 16-23-50(A)(2). If you have the handgun concealed, you are also subject to prosecution under South Carolina Code of Laws Section 16-23-460 that is a misdemeanor with the potential penalty of a fine between $200 and $500, a jail stay between 30 and 90 days, and the mandatory forfeiture of your weapon to the government. One bright spot is that a conviction will not burden you with a Federal firearms disability.

So, you cannot walk around with a pistol on your hip or concealed in your clothes unless you legally possess and carry under an exception. In general, possession is a broader category that extends from having the handgun in the building or vehicle that you occupy whereas carrying is narrower such as in your clothes or purse/backpack.

A handgun is described as, "any firearm designed to expel a projectile and designed to be fired from the hand, but shall not include any firearm generally recognized or classified as an antique, curiosity, or collector's item, or any that does not fire fixed cartridges." That sentence is a mouthful. Generally speaking, it means pistols and revolvers that you would have on hand to shoot and not collect as a hobby. This Chapter, and a good portion of this book, is designed to explain the exceptions.

Handguns in Your Home

Under South Carolina Code of Laws Section 16-23-20(8), you can carry a handgun, concealed or open, in your home. The main restriction is that it must be legal for you to own the gun in the first place. So, if you are legally entitled to own a handgun, you can watch TV or cook dinner inside your home with that gun on your hip or in your pocket. You can also carry the same handgun, concealed or not, on your entire outside premises if you own the land and buildings around your home. Also, even if you do not own the dwelling you are in but have legal control of that dwelling, you have the same right to carry as if you were the owner. For instance, if you have a valid lease at an apartment complex, you have legal control over your dwelling unit.

If you live in an apartment, condominium or similarly attached residential dwelling unit, you are only entitled to carry in your unit and not around the common areas. There is one exception to this common areas prohibition though. You can carry a handgun in the common areas if you are walking *directly* from your dwelling to your vehicle. This privilege stems from South Carolina Code Section 16-23-20(15) that allows carry between a vehicle and a place where you are legally entitled to possess a handgun.

If it is safe to do so, you can even fire guns on your property. In fact, a case interpreting the Shooting Range Protection Act found that an area customarily used for shooting at a person's home property was protected from legal actions based upon nuisance for noise. Of course, always follow gun safety rules when shooting on your home property. Pay special attention to the chapter on common gun crimes and lawsuits so that you understand possible criminal and civil liability regarding discharging guns.

Handguns and Firearms in Foster Homes

If you have foster children in your home, there are special rules for you. Section 114-550(H)(18) of the South Carolina Code of Regulations requires that firearms (including handguns) and any ammunition shall be kept in a locked storage container except when being legally carried upon the foster parent's person. There are other exceptions also. A firearm and ammunition can be out of the locked storage container if it is being used for educational, recreational, or defense of self or property purposes by the foster parent. A foster parent can also have the firearm out for cleaning. Note that this provision applies whether the foster parents have a concealed weapons permit or not.

Handguns in Other People's Homes with Permission

Under South Carolina Code of Laws Section 16-23-20(8), you can carry a handgun on the premises and inside of other people's homes if you have their permission to be on the premises and have their permission to possess a handgun on the premises. So, if you are at your grandparent's beach house on Edisto Beach and want to have a handgun there, you fall within the exception and can carry on the premises or inside the beach house. This assumes that you have your grandparent's permission to be on the premises and their permission to possess a handgun on the premises. Similarly, if you regularly go to a friend's apartment and he allows you to be on the premises and to have a handgun there, you are within the exception and can possess. Again, this applies whether you have a concealed weapons permit or not.

Group Child Care Homes

Group child homes are private homes designed and licensed to provide education or supervision of children. South Carolina Code of Regulations 114-517(E)(3) requires that firearms, weapons, and ammunition (in group child care homes) are to be kept in a locked drawer or cabinet.

Child Care Centers

With or without a concealed weapons permit, you cannot bring a firearm to any child care center. It makes no difference if the child care center is public, private or connected to a religious institution. Treat those places like you would a school. For all child care centers, 114-507(E)(3) provides that firearms, weapons, and ammunition are not permitted in the center or on the premises without the express permission of the authorities in charge of the premises or property. This does not apply to a guard, law enforcement officer, or member of the armed forces, or student of military science. Review the "Rules for Schools" section of this chapter for further clarification.

Business Owners Bringing Handguns to Work

(See the Guns at Work Chart in the Concealed Weapons Permit chapter for an easy reference guide for carry at work questions.)

Under Section 16-23-20(13) of the South Carolina Code of Laws, a business owner can carry a handgun, concealed or not, on the premises of his or her business. So, a baker can have a handgun on his hip while on the premises of his bakery. If he thinks wearing a handgun on his hip will scare-off customers, he can carry a handgun concealed, with or without a concealed weapons permit, on his premises. If he is in the suburbs and has a parking lot on his premises, he can carry in the parking lot. Alternatively, if his shop is downtown and he has only a city sidewalk outside of his door, his privilege ends at his door threshold.

There are two different definitions for a business owner under this business owner privilege. First, as discussed in the paragraph above, the privilege exists for the actual owner of the premises. Therefore, if you own the building and surrounding premises where you actively conduct your business, you have the privilege for the building and surrounding premises.

Second, the privilege exists for the person who has legal control of the business. Therefore, if you are leasing the building and premises from a landlord, the privilege exists for you in the building and the premises. For business owners who lease in a community commercial space such as malls, shopping centers and strip centers, the more restrictive rules that apply to the common areas for apartments controls. Therefore, business owners in stores with common areas like shopping centers should assume that their privilege stops at the front door threshold. These business owners should also be aware of lease provisions that may prohibit business owners from having guns on the premises. But while breaking terms or conditions of a lease might bring a breach of contract action against a business owner, the owner is not open to criminal prosecution by the government as a result of solely breaking the terms or conditions of a lease.

The second definition of business owner allows another possible privilege holder. Dr. Robert Butler, Vice President and Legislative Director of GrassRoots Gunrights of South Carolina, assisted in drafting the business owner privilege legislation. He indicates that the intent of the legislation is to extend the definition of "legal control of a business" to include the on-site manager or supervisor if the business is owned by a corporation since corporations are not human and can only act through humans. The privilege seems to cover only one manager or supervisor at any given time on the premises.

Defining Fixed Place of Business

South Carolina Code Section 16-23-20(13) provides for the foregoing privilege. However, that section also restricts the privilege to fixed places of business. Stores, restaurants, offices, manufacturing plants, malls, gas stations, and shopping centers are fixed places of business. Kiosks in malls are probably fixed if the business generally occupies the kiosk in the same place from day-to-day. Similarly, semi-permanent fruit stands and food huts are probably fixed if the stand generally occupies the same place from day-to-day and leases the land.

It is less likely that a court would find that wheeled businesses like boiled peanut trailers or barbeque smokers are fixed places of business unless they occupy the same place day-after-day. On the other hand, ice cream trucks that move through neighborhoods probably do not pass statutory muster for a fixed place of business. However, the ice cream man inside his truck is still privileged under the exception for vehicles. Although, if he is using the vehicle exception, he needs to have it in the glove box or other encased areas discussed below under the automobile exception. He cannot carry it as if it were a fixed place of business. The ice cream man scenario can be extrapolated for any similar mobile business arrangement that you can think of. Likewise, the semi-permanent fruit stand or food scenarios can be extrapolated for other similar business arrangements. We are not aware of cases determining what is, or is not, a fixed place of business for the purposes of Code Section 16-23-20(13). Therefore, we can only try to envision business arrangements that probably fall on one side or the other. For your practical purposes in trying to obey the law, the more that you attempt to stretch the meaning of "fixed place of business," the more chance you have of ending up a test court case on the subject. You do not want to be a test case under a criminal statute such as section 16-23-20(13) because conviction means jail time, fines and confiscation of the handgun.

Employees Bringing Handguns to Work

(See the Guns at Work Chart in the *Concealed Weapons Permit* chapter for an easy reference guide for carry at work questions.)

For employees of a business, other than a manager or supervisor of a corporation discussed above, the rules are different for handguns at work. As described in the CWP chapter, in order for employees to carry while at work, they must determine whether they can legally carry pursuant to their concealed weapons permit or pursuant to an exception to the general statutory handgun prohibition. In other words, there are two ways for an employee to legally carry at work but the employee must make sure that he or she falls under one of the two statutorily created exceptions.

One way an employee can legally carry at work is by carrying under a concealed weapons permit pursuant to South Carolina Code of Laws Section 16-23-20(12). Under this provision of the concealed weapons permit law, an employee can carry a concealable weapon, concealed into his work without first obtaining his employer's permission (and even knowledge). However, the employee cannot carry pursuant to a concealed weapons permit if the business sells alcoholic beer, wine or liquors for on-site consumption. Likewise, an employee cannot carry under the concealed weapons permit statute if the employer has erected a proper NO CONCEALED WEAPONS ALLOWED sign on the premises.

Another way an employee can carry at work is under the South Carolina Code of Laws Section 16-23-20(13) exception. Under this exception, an employee can carry any legal firearm at work, open or concealed, so long as the employee has the permission of the owner or person in legal control *and* has a concealed weapons permit. Even under this permissive exception, though, employees of a business that sells alcohol for on-site consumption cannot carry a pistol or firearm while on the business premises. Note that, even though carrying at work under this exception requires the employee to have a CWP, the employee is not carrying pursuant to the permit but pursuant to the statutory exception. Therefore, the employee may carry openly and may carry firearms different from those defined previously in this chapter as "concealable weapons." Further, an employee carrying under this statutory exception may carry at a business that posts the NO CONCEALED WEAPONS ALLOWED sign because the employee has the business owner's (or the person in legal control's) permission.

It is important for an employee to recognize the difference between the legal and business policy rules for guns at work. The above two statutory exceptions are legal rules for carrying a firearm at work. An employee's failure to carry properly pursuant to one of those two exceptions exposes the employee to criminal arrest and prosecution. Alternatively, the employee should also determine if the company has a firearm policy that would prevent him or her from possessing guns at work. If the company has a policy against employees carrying guns at work, the employee could face discipline or be fired regardless of what the statutes say about employees carrying firearms at work.

Handguns at Businesses that Serve Alcohol

Regardless of whether a business owner (or the person in legal control of a business as described above) has a permit or not, he or she can carry a handgun, openly or concealed, at his or her place of business. This privilege comes directly from South Carolina Code Section 16-23-20(13) and is not abated by additional language in the section, any other code section, or case law. For more analysis on guns and businesses that serve alcohol, see the concealed weapons permit chapter. However, Section 16-23-20(13) contains additional language that restricts employees from carrying handguns at businesses that serve alcohol for on-site consumption.

For businesses that sell liquor, beer, or wine for on premises consumption, employees of those businesses cannot use the employee privilege of Section 16-23-20(13). Remember that Section 16-23-20(13) gives employees the privilege to carry a concealable weapon if they have a concealed weapons permit and the permission of the owner. The same section explicitly removes the employee privilege for employees while working at a business that serves alcohol for onsite consumption. Therefore, if you are an employee of a business that serves alcohol, whether they are serving alcohol or not while you are there, you cannot carry a concealable weapon on the premises. (Again, the rules for carrying guns at work are organized in the "Guns at Work" chart in chapter 5.)

Who can carry a handgun onto the premises of a business that serves alcohol?

Again, the business owner or person in legal control of the business, concealed or not, with or without a permit. The same person can even drink alcohol while possessing the handgun. Further, the owner or person in legal control can lawfully use the handgun while intoxicated if the handgun is used in self-defense as described in the chapter on self-defense.

South Carolina state, local and reserve law enforcement officers can carry a weapon, concealed or not, onto a business that serves alcohol for consumption on the premises. According to an Attorney General Opinion dated May 12, 2006, the officer does not have to be uniformed or furthering his or her official duties. However, federal or out-of-state law enforcement officers must be furthering official duties. Every officer, though, should check with the policy of their department regarding carrying off-duty.

89

Automobiles and Other Private Conveyances

If you do not have a concealed weapons permit and you are
traveling within South Carolina, you can have a handgun in your car or
other conveyance under the handgun exception found in Section 16-
23-20(9)(a) of the South Carolina Code of Laws. A conveyance is any
vehicle used to get you down the road. Traveling in a car or other
conveyance from one location in South Carolina to a destination in
South Carolina keeps you under the state law that we are discussing
here. For traveling between states, we discuss the interstate rules a little
later in this chapter.

The basic rule is that you can carry a loaded handgun in your
vehicle if it is secured in a closed glove compartment, a closed console,
or in the trunk. You may also transport the handgun if it is in a closed
container secured by an integral fastener and if that container is in the
luggage compartment. It is legal to open the glove compartment,
console, or trunk in order to retrieve a driver's license, registration, or
proof of insurance for a law enforcement officer. Again, be very careful
if you have a gun in your vehicle and you are stopped by a law
enforcement officer. The first thing that you should do (before
reaching for anything) is inform the officer that you have a firearm and
tell him or her where it is located. Ask the officer if he or she would
like for you to get your license and registration or if the officer would
like to retrieve it. Let the officer direct you on how to act.

Vehicle Trunks vs. SUV Luggage Compartments

Many automobiles built today do not have a trunk but, rather,
have a luggage compartment towards the rear of the vehicle. For
instance, most SUVs have a storage area behind the last row of seats
towards the rear of the vehicle. The statutes provide that a handgun
may be kept in a vehicle if it is secured in a closed glove compartment,
closed console, closed trunk, or in a closed container secured by an

integral fastener and transported in the luggage compartment of the vehicle. You might ask, what is the luggage compartment? Thankfully, the statutes answer that question.

Luggage compartment means the trunk of a motor vehicle which has a trunk; however, with respect to a motor vehicle which does not have a trunk, the luggage compartment is the area of the motor vehicle in which the manufacturer designed that luggage be carried or to the area of the motor vehicle in which luggage is customarily carried. In a station wagon, van, hatchback vehicle, or sport utility vehicle, the luggage compartment is the area behind, but not under, the rearmost seat. In a truck, the luggage compartment is the area behind the rearmost seat, but not under the front seat.

If you keep the handgun in the luggage compartment, it must be in a closed container secured by an integral fastener. A closed container is best defined as a relatively strong container that is capable of fully encasing the handgun and closing completely with a handgun inside. Integral fastener is a latch or lock that is designed to be a functioning element of the container and capable of keeping the container closed and the contents inside the container. Think of a closed container with an integral fastener in terms of a commercially available clasping case. The case does not need to be locking in the sense of a padlock or combination lock but, rather, clasping in the sense of gun case latches, fishing tackle box clasps, or an ice cooler snap straps. At the subcommittee hearing where this issue was discussed, it was determined that a zippered gun rug (or nylon case) and a hard plastic gun case with clasps are good examples of qualifying containers. The easiest way to insure compliance is to buy a commercially available gun container at your local gun store.

91

Guns on the Seat, Floor or Door Pocket of a Car

For convenience or whatever reason, some people might be inclined to leave or place a handgun on the seat or the floor of their car, boat or other conveyance. Except for possibly under the Fishing or Hunting exceptions founds in Section 16-23-20(4), with or without a permit, it is not lawful in South Carolina to have a handgun under the front seat of a vehicle. Also, with or without a permit, you cannot keep a handgun on the seat or in a door pocket of the vehicle. The best way to stay safe from criminal and civil liability is to keep handguns in safe containers like holsters, purses, pockets, cases or glove compartments. Do not leave handguns lying around the car somewhere. Treat handguns like the deadly weapons that they are and not like you would a bag of cheese doodles.

Traveling Out of South Carolina

Say that you want to travel outside of the State of South Carolina for a family reunion. If your family gatherings are anything like ours, you will want to take your gun to defend your plate of food. Seriously though, gun owners want to bring their gun with them at all times and traveling is no exception. The problem is that different states have different laws with regard to guns. Slightly out of character, the Federal Government has provided some gun protection for interstate travelers. 18 USC Section 923(A), also known as the Firearm Owners' Protection Act or "FOPA," provides:

> Notwithstanding any other provision of any law or any rule or regulation of the State or any political subdivision thereof, any person who is not otherwise prohibited by this chapter from transporting, shipping, or receiving a firearm shall be entitled to transport a firearm for any lawful purpose from any place where he may lawfully possess and carry such firearm to any other place where he may lawfully possess and carry such firearm if, during such transportation the

firearm is unloaded, and neither the firearm nor any ammunition being transported is readily accessible or is directly accessible from the passenger compartment of such transporting vehicle: provided, that in the case of a vehicle without a compartment separate from the driver's compartment the firearm or ammunition shall be contained in a locked container other than the glove compartment or console.

Does the Federal Law Protect You?

So, FOPA sounds pretty good, but before you throw the gun into the car and take off, consider the limitations of this law. First, you must be a person who is not otherwise prohibited from transporting, shipping, or receiving a firearm. In other words, you must not be prohibited from possessing a firearm. We help you determine whether or not you are prohibited from possessing a firearm in several other parts of this book so we will not revisit any of those analyses here.

If you are not prohibited from possessing a firearm, you move on to the next phase of analysis. You must determine if it is legal for you to both posses AND carry the firearm in both the departure state AND the destination state. To simplify this analysis you can focus on the carry portion of the analysis. This is true because, in order to carry a gun you must, by definition, also possess the gun. This means there is no instance where you could carry a gun without possessing it. Therefore if it is legal to carry it, then it is also legal to possess it.

Carrying Pursuant to a CWP and Reciprocity

Before going further, now is a good time to discuss another benefit of getting your concealed weapons permit (CWP). You do not have to worry about the rules of the FOPA if you have a South Carolina CWP and you are in a state with reciprocity. If you have your CWP and are in a state that has reciprocity with South Carolina, you can carry your gun concealed so long as you carry under the rules of that state's CWP law. If you are traveling through several states, all of which have reciprocity with South Carolina, you do not have to mind the provisions of the FOPA because you will be carrying pursuant to your permit. However, you must know and follow the rules for concealed carry in each individual state. In general, most states have minor differences in concealed weapons permit rules but you are responsible for the difference none-the-less. To understand the differences in reciprocity states, check each state's website or law enforcement agency. Also, Alan Korwin of Bloomfield Press (gunlaws.com) has books on the subject that might be of assistance to you. Please note that the authors make no implied or express warranty or recommendation of those reference materials.

Interstate Travel Scenarios under the FOPA

To help you understand how to best travel interstate under the FOPA, it is helpful to discuss scenarios that you might encounter. An easily understood scenario is one in which you have a South Carolina CWP and you are traveling from a point of origin in South Carolina, through one or more reciprocity states and ultimately to a state that has reciprocity with South Carolina. As discussed in the previous section, it is legal for you to possess and carry the gun in your departure state (South Carolina) and it is legal for you to possess and carry the gun in accordance with each state's CWP rules in each state that you travel through and in the destination state. You do not have to mind the FOPA rules under this scenario, only the rules for carry under a CWP for each state that you are in. Alternatively, you can choose not to carry under the CWP rules but, rather, follow the FOPA rules. The advantage of traveling this way is that you only have to know how to travel pursuant to the FOPA and you are not required to know the CWP carry rules for each state of travel. The disadvantage is that you will probably not be able to have your firearm on or about your person during travel and possibly when you get to your destination state.

Another easily understood scenario would be where you are not allowed to possess and carry a firearm at all in either the state of origin or the destination state. If it is unlawful for you to possess and carry the gun in both the departure state and the destination state, you cannot transport firearms under the FOPA.

A slightly more complicated scenario would be that you have a South Carolina CWP and are traveling to a destination state that has reciprocity with South Carolina. However, you are also traveling through one or more states that do not have reciprocity with South Carolina. Under this scenario, you are only allowed to carry under your CWP in the reciprocity states but must travel under the rules of the FOPA in the non-reciprocity states.

Scenarios other than those described above are less clear-cut and place you in a legal grey area. Questions arise if you are legal to carry the gun under limited circumstances in either the departure state or the destination state. Typical examples are that many states allow you to carry a gun if you are hunting, fishing, or going to a shooting range or other lawful shooting function. If you are not going to one of these activities in the destination state, this can make the FOPA inapplicable. Further complicating the analysis is the fact that generally, this Federal law will be interpreted by a state court. The way that the FOPA normally comes up is where someone is traveling and gets stopped by a member of the state or local police force. The person is charged on state gun violations and gets tried in a state court. As a result of our judicial structure under Federalism, unless the United States Supreme Court steps in, the provisions of FOPA will be decided by state courts. State courts may view some of the nuances of FOPA differently. That being said, the following information can be used to make the best choice on whether or not you can transport your gun and, if so, under what circumstances.

To illustrate the difficulty of determining what a court will decide when it comes to state guns laws and FOPA, let us look at a case out of the State of New York. _Beach v. Kelly_ involves the interpretation of FOPA by a New York state court. This case involves a citizen of New York (Beach) who worked in private security and obtained a license which is known as a _Premises Resident Pistol License_. This is a restricted license that applies only to a specific location. It also allows the person to transport the pistol as long as it is unloaded, secured in a locked container, and transported only to and from authorized small arms ranges and shooting clubs. (This same freedom to exercise the natural right to keep and bear arms exists in many states without any licenses at all.) Through an unrelated investigation, the licensing body in New York learned that Mr. Beach transported his gun to the State of Nevada for a security officer convention. New York used Beach's action as a basis to revoke his Premises Resident Pistol License.

Mr. Beach appealed the decision to a New York court and initially won. The trial court found that the word _carry_ as used in the FOPA should not be construed so narrowly as to undercut the Act's basic objective. The court was following the guidance provided by the U.S. Supreme Court case _Muscarello v. United States_. The trial court further noted that in _City of Camden v. Beretta_, the US Supreme Court determined that the basic objective of the FOPA was to allow law abiding citizens the right to transport their firearms in a safe manner during interstate travel.

Unfortunately for Mr. Beach, the decision of the trial court was overturned on appeal. The New York Supreme Court determined that Mr. Beach's license allowed him to carry the firearm on the specific premises listed in the license. The Court found that the license only allowed Mr. Beach to carry the firearm away from that location if he was going to a small arms range or shooting club or hunting area. The New York Supreme Court determined that, since Mr. Beach was not taking the gun to a small arms shooting range, shooting club, or hunting area, it was not legal for him to leave the premises with the gun. Further, since it was not legal for him to leave the premises with the gun, under the circumstances at the time he left the premises, the FOPA did not apply.

While that is a lot to digest, the main point is that you should be careful if you plan to travel interstate under the FOPA. There are a number of technical requirements in order to be protected by the Act and state courts sometimes stretch the Act's plain meaning. However, the following section should give you enough information to analyze your travels and determine if the Act will protect you.

Defining Destination States

In order for the Act to apply, you cannot be prohibited from possessing and carrying the gun in the destination state. More accurately, you must not be prohibited from possessing and carrying a firearm in *each and every* destination states. Yes, you can have more than one destination state. So, what is a destination state?

The answer is easy to determine if you drive non-stop from your state of origin to your destination state, stay in the destination state for a week and then drive non-stop back to your origin state. In that scenario, your destination states are clearly defined. It becomes less clear if you make any legally significant stops in any of the states between those states. Courts have determined that stopping for gas and food in a non-destination state does not create a sufficient intent to make that state a destination state. Likewise, courts have determined that renting a motel for the night in a non-destination state is not evidence of intent to make that state a destination state. However, if you stop and visit a theme park in what you consider a non-destination state, courts are likely consider that stop sufficient evidence of an intent to make that a destination state. Similarly, meeting a client or doing any business in a state will almost certainly be sufficient evidence of intent to make that state a destination state for purposes of the FOPA.

Rules for Transporting Interstate under the FOPA

Once you have determined each destination state and that you are not prohibited from possessing and carrying in that state, you can then legally transport firearms according to the FOPA. To be protected by the Act, you must transport firearms unloaded AND both the firearms and any ammunition must not be readily accessible from the passenger compartment. In plain English, you should keep the unloaded firearms and ammunition in the trunk. If the vehicle does not have a trunk, the unloaded firearms and ammunition should be kept separate in locked containers in a place *other than* the glove compartment or console.

Also, it must be legal for you to possess and carry the gun in your *destination* state. Notice that it must be legal for you to possess a gun in the state you are going to and not just South Carolina. Again, the gun must be unloaded and both the gun and the ammo must be stored in such a way that they are not directly or readily accessible. In other words, the gun should be unloaded and carried in your trunk. If your vehicle does not have a trunk, and no other section that is separate from the passenger compartment, it must be stored in a locked container but not the glove box or the console. Locked here does not mean padlocked or combination locked but rather that the integral locking mechanism is closed. Again, a better word to describe a locked integral locking mechanism might be *latched*.

Federal law allows you to transport your gun *through* whichever states in the United States you desire. As you travel through each state, you are free to carry your weapon to the extent that state permits. For example, if you are traveling through a state with the same possession laws as South Carolina, you can take your gun out of the trunk and put it into your glove box or console. When you get to the next state line, you must reevaluate where you are allowed to keep the gun.

Motorcycles

Without a permit, the most important thing to remember about motorcycles is that the handgun must be secured inside of a compartment. Under Section 16-23-20(16) of the South Carolina Code of Laws, you can legally carry a handgun inside a saddlebag, side compartment, or rear compartment so long as the compartment can be securely closed.

Private Boats

The best way to possess or carry a firearm on a boat is by using the hunting and fishing exception found in Section 16-23-20(4) of the South Carolina Code of Laws. That section provides an exception for "licensed hunters or fishermen who are engaged in hunting or fishing or going to or from their places of hunting or fishing while in a vehicle or on foot." Therefore, you can possess or carry a handgun, whether openly or concealed, so long as you have a fishing license and are fishing or going to or from a place of fishing. If you want to carry or possess under this exception while going to or from a place of fishing, make sure that you are going *directly* to or from the place of fishing. Remember that this exception applies to and from a place where it is legal to possess or carry a handgun (such as your home or vehicle) to the place of fishing. This exception only applies if the person possessing or carrying the handgun has a valid hunting or fishing license AND is engaged in hunting or fishing at the time of possessing or carrying the handgun. The Section 16-23-20(4) exception is applicable to all rivers, lakes, ponds and water bodies that you will encounter in or abutting South Carolina lands.

While the authors have not been able to find a definitive legal authority on this, the best practice is to assume that South Carolina law applies at least 3 miles out into the Atlantic. After that, you are in international waters and there are no gun restrictions against most common semi-automatic rifles, pistols and revolvers. Be careful, though, if you plan to arrive at a foreign nation like Bermuda or the Bahamas with your vessel. Once you get into their waters, you are under their laws. Also, make sure your guns are legal before you come back into the waters of the state of South Carolina. A detailed discussion of firearms on the seas is beyond the scope of this book so you are advised to look for more resources if you plan to be on the seas with a firearm.

Aircraft and Airports

Your ability to carry a firearm onto an aircraft depends upon variables such as your destination, whether the flight is private or commercial, the place in which you must embark and disembark the aircraft, the manner in which you wish to carry the firearm, and whether or not you have a CWP. We will first look at how you intend to carry the firearm. Remember that this discussion assumes that you are otherwise lawfully entitled to possess a firearm. Also remember that the regulations that we discuss here originate in federal law so violations are federal offenses.

We can start by determining whether you plan to be in the sterile area or only in non-sterile areas of the airports. Several different federal statutes and regulations apply to transportation of firearms on aircraft, depending upon the type of aircraft and aircraft operation and where you board the aircraft.

The so-called *sterile area* of an airport is defined in 49 Code of Federal Regulations (CFR) 1540.5 as *a portion of an airport defined in the airport security program that provides passengers access to boarding aircraft and to which the access generally is controlled by TSA, or by an aircraft operator under part 1544 of this chapter or a foreign air carrier under part 1546 of this chapter, through the screening of persons and property.* So, the sterile areas are those places beginning at the entrance to the security checkpoints and up to, and including, the gates to the aircraft. The sterile area is easy to recognize because you first must subject yourself and your carry-on luggage to search and inspection before entering.

Upon entering the sterile area, you are subject to the prohibitions of 49 CFR 1540.111. This section prohibits carrying weapons on your person or in carry-on luggage or otherwise accessible. The section also prohibits weapons on board the aircraft that you board from a sterile area.

The section does provide a general exception for law enforcement officers that are required to carry firearms or other weapons while in the performance of law enforcement duties at the airport and virtually all other sworn law enforcement officers (49 CFR 1540.111(b)(1) and 1544.219). Other specific exceptions include law enforcement officers accompanying prisoners (49 CFR 1544.221), air marshals (49 CFR 1544.223), and employees of qualified private security service companies. Additional information regarding these exceptions is beyond the scope of this book so it is important for those seeking to carry under these exceptions to find materials that thoroughly discuss these sections of the CFR and federal statutes.

When it comes time to board an aircraft after leaving the sterile area, it does not matter whether the aircraft that you board is a commercial, charter, freight or private aircraft as a result of the broad prohibition from carrying a weapon onto the plane found in 49 CFR 1550.5. So, even if you are boarding a friend's private Cessna and you have his permission, it is unlawful for you to carry a firearm onto the plane if you enter through the sterile area.

Just because you cannot carry any weapon on your person or in your carry-on luggage, you still can take your firearm on your travels if it is otherwise legal to do so. Section 49 CFR 1540.111(c) permits passengers to pack firearms into checked luggage. You must first unload the firearm and declare the firearm to the airline or aircraft operator. You must keep the firearm locked in a hard-sided container and you must be the only person with the key or combination while in the sterile area or on the plane.

You can carry ammunition in checked-in luggage inside the locked hard-sided container with the firearm or on its own 49 CFR 1540.111(d). More specific information regarding carrying ammunition is contained in 49 CFR 175.10(a)(8). That section provides that ammunition must be securely packaged in boxes or other packages specifically designed to carry small amounts of ammunition and that ammunition clips and magazines must also be securely boxed. If you are flying a commercial airline or charter, you should check with that individual operator to get information about possible additional policies regarding firearms and ammunition.

Under Section 49 CFR 175.10(a)(9), you can carry mace or similar pepper spray onto commercial aircraft but you can only have one container and the container cannot hold more than 4 fluid ounces in volume. Further, the container must have a positive means to prevent accidental discharge and must be checked-in so that the aircraft operator can store the container in the luggage area of the aircraft.

A detailed discussion of the penalties for violations of these regulations is beyond the scope of this book. However, 49 USC §46505 makes it a crime, subject to fine and jail time for not more than 10 years, or both, when an individual on, or attempting to get on, an aircraft in, or intended for operation in, air transportation or intrastate air transportation, has on or about him a concealed dangerous weapon that is or would be accessible in flight. Additionally,

49 USC §46303 provides for a civil penalty of $10,000 for having a concealed dangerous weapon that is or would be accessible to the individual in flight.

Carrying a firearm in the non-sterile areas is less burdened with federal regulations than in sterile areas but there are some significant rules that you are required to follow under federal law. In the non-sterile areas, your ability to possess a firearm will depend upon factors like: the way you are carrying the firearm, the size of the aircraft, your destination, and whether the flight is commercial or private. As before, you must be otherwise carrying lawfully under South Carolina law as explained in other sections of this book.

While 49 USC §46505 above seems to criminalize firearms on virtually all aircraft, the definitions of *air transportation* and *intrastate air transportation* found in 49 USC §40102 limit the applicability of the statute to *commercial air carriers*. Air carriers are defined as individuals or businesses that provide transportation for hire either between 2 states or within 1 state using a turbojet aircraft with more than 30 seats. So, for the most part, these definitions limit the applicability of this statute to the airlines and charter businesses that are conducting flights between states or flying with 31 seat and larger turbojet aircraft.

In concert with 49 USC §46505, 49 CFR 1550.7 provides a blanket prohibition of firearms (except for the previously discussed exceptions) on aircraft weighing more than 12,500 pounds and where the aircraft's operation is not otherwise subject to the statutes and regulations addressed above. Under this regulation, the aircraft operator must conduct a search of the aircraft before departure and screen all passengers, crewmembers, and other persons and their carry-on items before boarding regardless of whether boarding and loading occurs from a sterile area.

Under 14 CFR 135.119, charter flights have specific firearms restrictions. Under this regulation, you may not, while on board an aircraft being operated by a [charter flight] certificate holder, carry on or about you a deadly or dangerous weapon, either concealed or not concealed. This section does not apply to many law enforcement officers or to crew members who have their company's permission to carry firearms. So, while this regulation appears to limit the possession of firearms, if the charter operator grants you permission, either directly or though their general policy, you are excepted from the regulation and able to carry firearms onboard.

You are under no federal regulations if you are flying in a private aircraft not being operated by a common carrier within South Carolina. If you are flying between South Carolina and another state, you are subject to 18 USC §926(A) just as if you were driving or otherwise traveling interstate. For a more detailed description of interstate travel under 18 USC §926, see the *Traveling Out of South Carolina* section earlier in this chapter.

Public Transportation

If you have your Concealed Weapons Permit, you can carry in accordance with the CWP Statute. However, if you do not have a CWP, the rules are different for you. If you are riding on a bus, train or other type of public transportation vehicle within South Carolina without a CWP, you must ensure that your handgun, or any other weapon, is securely encased and stored in the locked trunk or luggage area as if you were in a private automobile or other conveyance. As always, encase it securely and store it safely.

If you are traveling to another state, federal rules apply and you need to have the weapon unloaded and in a locked container. You must also declare the weapon to the carrier company and deliver it to

the possession of the carrier for transportation. You must also comply
with the FOPA law discussed earlier in this Chapter.

The Rules for Schools

Do not carry a handgun, or any firearm, onto a school, college,
or university campus. South Carolina Code of Laws Sections 16-23-420
generally prohibits firearms on school grounds and events even with a
concealed weapons permit. All levels of schools from kindergarten to
universities are included in that section's prohibition. Further, all areas
of the school, not only inside the buildings, are no gun zones. Be aware
that the prohibition is for private schools as well as public schools and
even extends to preschools. It if resembles an institution for teaching
and learning, treat is like it is a school and do not bring a firearm with
you unless you have the correct permission (discussed later).

Criminal Penalties for Guns on School Grounds

The prohibition against guns at schools found in South
Carolina Code of Laws Sections 16-23-420 and 16-23-430 are virtually
identical yet are two separate offenses. Section 16-23-430 is somewhat
broader in that it prohibits all weapons which may be used to cause
bodily injury or death (guns certainly) but narrower in that it only
applies to elementary and secondary (middle and high) school grounds.
Therefore, if you bring a gun onto elementary or secondary school
grounds, and you do not fall within one of the exceptions, you can be
charged under **BOTH** Section 16-23-420 and 16-23-430. A violation of
Section 16-23-420 is a felony with the penalty of a fine of not more
than $5,000 or imprisonment of not more than 5 years, or both. A
violation of Section 16-23-430 is a felony with the penalty of a fine of
not more than $1,000 or imprisonment of not more than 5 years, or
both. Under Section 16-23-430, the arresting agency can confiscate the
gun. A conviction under either of these sections subjects you to a
lifetime federal firearms disability. If the gun is concealed you can tack

on a Section 16-23-460 violation that is a misdemeanor with the penalty of a $200-$500 fine or a jail term of 30-90 days and a mandatory forfeiture of the gun to the government. Section 16-23-420 is explained in greater detail below in the *No Deadly Weapons on Elementary and Secondary School Grounds* section later in this chapter.

As in the CWP chapter, it should be noted that federal law allows a South Carolina CWP holder to carry in schools and on school grounds, but it is South Carolina law that makes it illegal for a CWP holder to drop-off or pick-up his or her children from school while armed even if the firearm never leaves the vehicle. Therefore, South Carolina law is more restrictive than federal law in this area. South Carolina's more restrictive law places a great burden on law abiding parents that want to keep a gun with them but also must enter school grounds to pick-up or drop-off their kids. Please contact your representative and demand that South Carolina change this burdensome and completely unnecessary and illogical restriction.

Getting back to the prohibition of guns on school grounds, be cautioned that this prohibition extends to **any** properties owned by the school or university, too. So, if a tract of land somewhere in the boonies is donated or willed to a college, innocent hunters or explorers that may traipse across the land are committing a felony. There is no requirement that the person with the firearm know the unimproved land he is on is actually owned by a school. If you are ever charged with violating this area of the Code but you had no knowledge that you were on such lands, your attorney might be able to raise some defenses such as mistake of fact. However, prevailing on such defenses is an uphill battle.

Off Campus Events

You are also prohibited from possessing a firearm at off-campus events sponsored by the school. Therefore, firearms are prohibited at school sponsored ball games, exhibitions, events, and programs. The prohibition applies even if the school does not own or lease the property on which the event is taking place. A school could be holding games on a privately owned field and you are prohibited from possessing a firearm at the event or in the parking area of the event. What you must keep in mind is, if the event that you are going to is a school sponsored event, with or without a concealed weapons permit, you cannot bring a firearm.

Driving Through a Campus

You are, however, entitled to transport or possess firearms and any other legal weapons on major state, county or city streets through or adjacent to school properties and events. Be aware though that, as soon as you pass over from the major street into a school road or parking lot, the prohibition applies.

Section 16-23-420(E) indicates that the road must be open "full-time" to public vehicular traffic. So, a road that is not open to public vehicular traffic 24 hours a day is technically off-limits to firearms possession or carry.

Be careful about state and local roads through campus that are not open 24 hours a day. For instance, a school might have authority to close a major road for a certain portion of the day for student parking or passenger drop-off.

What makes this language of the statute especially troubling is the likelihood that a vehicle operator is unaware whether a road is closed for a portion of the day. For instance, a gun owner or possessor from Augusta might be required to travel to Columbia for a meeting. That traveler might be driving on a road through the University of South Carolina that is closed for a portion of the day. Technically, the traveler is violating the law and is subject to serious criminal liability.

Exception for Permission from Authorities in Charge of the Premises

The foregoing is the general rule found in Section 16-23-420(A). That is, with or without a permit, no firearms at any school or any school event. We will next go through the very narrow exceptions to this very serious prohibition of firearms at schools.

The first exception is found in Section 16-23-420(A) itself. If you have the permission of the "authorities in charge of the premises or property," you can lawfully possess or carry a firearm onto a school, college or university. (This exception was probably created for school shooting matches and there are very few other instances where a school principal or president is likely to give you permission.) The statute does not explicitly define who these "authorities" are nor have the authors been able to uncover any court cases that define the terminology. Therefore, we are left with simply trying to give you our best interpretation of the terms.

The term "authorities" is plural so it can be inferred that there is more than one source of authority from which to obtain the permission. Further, the statute references the authority "in charge" so some sort of administrator can be inferred. Finally, the statute specifically references "premises or property" so it can be inferred that the statute contemplates the person or persons in charge of the specific property where the firearm will be allowed.

So, we can reasonably infer that "authorities in charge" include the school president or principal, a campus police chief, grounds or physical plant chief, superintendent of schools, school board, school board chief, or similar administrator with managerial authority.

Because the statute references the "premises or property," it can be inferred that the person that gives permission must have authority over the actual property to be entered with a firearm. So, the permission is arguably sufficient if it is obtained from an authority that is in charge of the property that the firearm is brought upon even if that authority is not the ultimate school authority like the president, principal or school board. For instance, a coach might have authority over a property that contains archery fields that are also sometimes used for shooting matches. The statute can be interpreted to define the coach as an "authority in charge of the premises or property."

The best form of permission is in writing so try to get that if you want to assure that you are legal. The worst type of permission would be to assume that you have permission when in fact you do not.

If you do get permission from an authority, beware that Section 16-23-420(B) makes it a crime for you to display, brandish or threaten anyone with a firearm at a school. Therefore, you could get a criminal charge for showing off or threatening someone with a firearm. While it is impossible to use a firearm at a school shooting match without displaying it or brandishing it, it seems ridiculous that you would get prosecuted under this seemingly incongruent statutory language. On the other hand, it seems very likely that you would get prosecuted under the statute if you were threatening someone with a firearm at a shooting match at school.

Exception for Law Enforcement and Guards

Section 16-23-420(D) exempts authorized guards and law enforcement officers. Guard is not defined by the statute or related case law so we will assume the statute means private *security officers* hired by the school or stationed at the school with the school official's permission. Guard probably also means armored vehicle security officers on campus to service ATMs and financial institutions. For more information on security officer definitions and licensure in South Carolina, see the chapter on miscellaneous gun laws later in this book.

Notwithstanding the relatively ambiguous statutory meaning of *guard*, it is clear that all law enforcement officers are exempted. Remember that most campus police are state pay-rolled law enforcement officers and not private security officers.

Exception for Military and Military Science

Less clear is the exception for members of the armed forces and students of military science found in South Carolina Code of Laws Section 16-23-420(D). In the practical sense, these students primarily exhibit firearms on campus for drills and the firearms are typically nonfunctional. Some college programs might have live-fire shooting competitions at gun ranges or remote and secured areas of the school. In an abundance of caution as a result of a lack of controlling court decisions, the best advice for members of the armed forces and military science on campus is to never possess a firearm on campus except when provided by your command for official purposes. Otherwise, you are risking a felony charge and all of the wonderful civil rights deprivations that go along with it.

Exception for Married Students

Another exception is for married students found in Section 16-23-420(D) of the South Carolina Code of Laws. Married students residing in an apartment provided by the private or public school can carry a firearm in or around a particular building if authorized by the person legally responsible for the security of the buildings. Your likelihood of getting such permission is probably slim but the exception does exist in the statutes. The married exception is somewhat of a statutory oddity. Why would the legislature carve out a special exception for married people living on campus? One reason might be as an incentive for students to get married. Talk about a shotgun wedding! Another reason might be to create an incentive for married couples with guns to consider living on campus. Additionally puzzling is that the exception is really not an exception at all. Married or not, part (A) of Section 16-23-420 requires that any student desiring to have a firearm on campus first get permission from campus officials.

For the Military, Military Science, or married student exceptions, unless you are a law enforcement officer or qualified guard you will need written permission from the campus police chief or the university president. You will probably get denied but there is no law against asking.

If you are a hunter, many college police departments allow you to keep your hunting rifles and possibly hunting pistols at the police station. Get permission from the campus police department first though before bringing the firearm on campus.

No Deadly Weapons on Elementary and Secondary School Grounds

In addition to the general prohibition of firearms on school premises and events without permission from authorities in charge of the premises, Section 16-23-430 makes it a crime to possess or carry *any* weapon onto the premises of any elementary or secondary school without the permission of school officials. The statute lists knives (with a blade over two inches long), blackjacks, metal pipes or poles, or any other type of weapon, device or object which may be used to inflict bodily injury or death. Therefore, just about anything that can be used as a dangerous or deadly weapon is prohibited on elementary or secondary (middle and high) school premises.

Anyone that looks at the above statute section should see that it is ridiculously over broad. Prohibited items include, "any other type of weapon, device or object that may be used to inflict bodily injury or death." Without even considering items on the school lunch menu, think of all the things students can use to inflict bodily injury or death on each other. Pens and pencils may be jabbed into the eyes. A backpack strap may be used as a garrote around the neck. A baseball bat may be cracked against the head. Quite literally, a jury could find most students, teachers and administrators in violation of this statute on any given school day.

It is unclear if the term *school officials* used in Section 16-23-430 differs from the meaning of *authorities in charge of the premises or property* described in Section 16-23-420. The term *school officials* might encompass a broader class of administrators that have school managerial responsibilities but are not necessarily in charge of the premises or property. However, the terms might be synonymous. The authors and legislative consultant are not aware of any case law interpreting these terms so we cannot give a more definite definition. So, the "Exception for Permission from the Authorities in Charge of the Premises" section of this chapter contains the best advice that we can give at this time.

Expulsion for Bringing a Firearm to a Public School

Section 59-63-235 of the South Carolina Code of Laws provides for the mandatory expulsion of any student determined to have brought a firearm to school. For the purposes of this section, *student* means a person enrolled in a public education institution so you should assume that this means public school students from preschools through universities. Under this section, the district board of trustees must expel the student for no less than one year if they determine that the student brought a firearm onto the school grounds or any setting under the jurisdiction of a local board of trustees. (Refer to the *Rules for Schools* section of this book for a more detailed discussion of the prohibition of firearms at schools.) The expulsion must follow the procedures established pursuant to South Carolina Code of Laws Section 59-63-240. The one-year expulsion is subject to modification by the district superintendent of education on a case-by-case basis. Students expelled pursuant to this section are not precluded from receiving educational services in an alternative setting. Each local board of trustees must establish a policy which requires the student to be referred to the local county office of the Department of Juvenile Justice or its representative.

Deadly Weapons, other than Firearms, at College

The prohibition against non-firearm weapons above is only directed at elementary, middle and high schools. The same prohibition does not extend to colleges and universities. Therefore, there is no prohibition against those non-firearm weapons listed above on college campuses. Just remember that there is a general prohibition from carrying those same weapons concealed on your person. Remember too, if you are a concealed weapons permit holder, a concealable weapon is defined as a firearm and the CWP statute does not grant an exception for CWP holders to carry firearms on school campuses.

Can I Carry on the Capitol Grounds in Columbia?

With or without a permit, Section 10-11-320 of the South Carolina Code of Laws makes it unlawful to discharge, carry, or otherwise have a firearm readily accessible while on the capitol grounds or within the capitol building. The section defines capitol grounds as, "that area inward from the vehicular traveled surfaces of Gervais, Sumter, Senate and Assembly Streets in the city of Columbia." If you violate this section you are guilty of a misdemeanor and, upon conviction, must be fined not more than $5,000 or imprisoned not more than 3 years, or both. Because this state misdemeanor has the potential for a jail sentence over 2 years, a person convicted of this crime will have a lifetime federal firearms disability in addition to the other penalties. Also, if the weapon was concealed, you are in violation of Section 16-23-460 and, if convicted, you will forfeit the firearm to the government forever.

There is somewhat of an exception for CWP holders. Section 10-11-320(B) provides that a CWP holder who is authorized to park on the capitol grounds or in the parking garage below the capitol grounds may have a firearm in the vehicle. However, the firearm must remain locked in the CWP holder's vehicle while on or below the capitol grounds and must be stored in a place in the vehicle that is not readily accessible to any person upon that person's entry to or below the capitol grounds. The best practice here is to place the firearm in the trunk or luggage compartment of the vehicle before entering the capitol grounds and then return it to any other legal location on your person or in the vehicle after you leave the capitol grounds.

Hotels, Motels and Lodging

With or without a permit, if you are otherwise legally entitled to possess one, you can have your firearm in your hotel room. Further, with or without the permit, you can carry the weapon concealed from your conveyance to your room. This authorization is found in Section 23-31-230 of the South Carolina Code of Laws. You must go directly from your conveyance to the room with the exception of check-in. Again, it is OK to have your concealed weapon with you while you check in but do not stop at the free continental breakfast, pool, or any other area unless you have your CWP. Never go into the bar even with a CWP.

South Carolina statute 45-2-30(A)(4) gives an innkeeper the right to refuse or deny anyone accommodations, facilities or privileges if the innkeeper reasonably believes that the guest is bringing onto the premises anything that might be dangerous to others. This statute specifically mentions firearms and explosives as potentially dangerous items. Therefore, this statue allows innkeepers to keep guests out if the innkeeper does not want firearms on the premises. This statute stands on its own and does not reference the "No concealable weapons allowed" sign discussed earlier.

However, for CWP holders, Section 45-2-30(A)(4) is in conflict with Section 23-31-203. The latter contains the language *not withstanding any provision of law* which overrides 45-2-30(A)(4) for persons carrying under the CWP Statute or carrying under another exception. So, CWP holders can carry a concealable weapon, concealed, from their conveyance to their lodging room or accommodation that they have rented and paid an accommodation tax upon. If you are not carrying according to the CWP statute, 45-2-30(A)(4) applies and an innkeeper might be justified in denying you accommodations, facilities or privileges if he thinks that you have a firearm and he does not want firearms on the premises. In that case, if you want to have your gun with you and the lodging business does not, just vote with your feet and check-in to a different lodging business.

There is a detail about Section 23-31-203 that you should be aware of. Again, that section reads, "any person may carry a concealable weapon from an automobile or other motorized conveyance to a room or other accommodation he has rented and upon which an accommodations tax has been *paid*. The verb "paid" indicates past tense so you are advised to pay for your accommodations in advance before arriving at the accommodations to take advantage of the provisions of this section.

National Parks, Forests and Wildlife Refuges

Through an executive order, the Bush Administration required that the director of U.S national parks create policies that are least restrictive to legal gun possessors. As a result, the Department of the Interior has promulgated a final rule allowing guns into national parks, forests and wildlife refuges consistent with each state's CWP law. Under the new rule, an individual is allowed to carry a concealed weapon in national parks, forests and wildlife refuges if, and only if, the individual is authorized to carry a concealed weapon under state law in the state in which the national park or refuge is located. Therefore, if you have a CWP, you can carry according to the CWP in one of these areas in any state where your CWP is valid.

Existing regulations regarding the carrying of firearms remain otherwise unchanged, particularly limitations on poaching and target practice and prohibitions on carrying firearms in federal buildings. Since buildings on these lands are federal buildings, your best practice is to not carry a firearm into buildings on these areas. The Department of the Interior has a very good website that has detailed information on every national park in the United States.

Hunting in National Forests

During hunting season, you can carry a handgun in a national forest if you have a hunting license. If it is not hunting season, you must get a permit from each county in which the forest is located. In order to get such a permit, you will need written permission from the park ranger in charge. Remember that South Carolina Section 16-23-20(4) additionally applies. This section makes it legal for hunters to have a handgun, openly or concealed, but only if they are licensed to hunt and are engaged in hunting or fishing or going to or from their places of hunting or fishing while in a vehicle or on foot.

Under the circumstances of the foregoing paragraph, you can carry a handgun, concealed or not, with or without a concealed weapons permit. As is the case with some of the other exceptions, if you are carrying under this exception but also have a concealed weapons permit, you are not required to present your CWP to a law enforcement officer if asked for ID from the officer.

State Forests and State Parks (There is a Difference!)

Firearms are prohibited within all state *parks* except in areas specifically designated for firearms. If you get a concealed weapons permit however, South Carolina Statute 51-3-145(G) exempts you from the firearms prohibition so you can bring your concealable weapon, concealed, into state parks. The South Carolina Department of Parks, Recreation and Tourism (SCDPRT) manages several quality gun ranges across the state. Obviously firearms are allowed in the gun range areas. If you do not have a permit and want to bring a handgun to use it at the gun range, here is our analysis of the law: Section 16-23-20(14) makes it legal for a person to have and use a handgun if the person is engaged in firearms-related activities while on the premises of a fixed place of business which conducts, as a regular course of its business, activities related to sale, repair, pawn, firearms training, or use of firearms. While not a business in the classic sense, a state park gun range appears to fit the definition of a fixed place of business that conducts the use of firearms as regular course of business. So, if it is legal for you to possess a handgun, you can likewise legally possess and use that handgun at a state park gun range.

Next, Section 16-23-20(15) makes it legal for a person while transferring a handgun directly from or to a vehicle and a location specified in this section where one may legally possess the handgun. As noted above, a gun range is a place where one may legally possess a handgun. Therefore, you can legally transport a handgun directly from your vehicle to the gun range in a state park. Again, whether coming or going, you must go directly between your vehicle and the range.

A word of caution, Section 16-23-20(14) makes it illegal for non-permit holders to have handguns in the state park if a sign limiting possession of firearms to holders of permits is posted. For the location of these gun ranges, check SCDPRT's website below.

For hunting in state *forests*, review the chapter on hunting and keep abreast of all current hunting regulations. SCDPRT regulates all South Carolina state forests and state parks. Their website is: www.southcarolinaparks.com and their general information phone number is: (803) 734-0156. The visitor information phone numbers are: (803) 734-1700 or toll free (866) 224-9339.

In general, be careful about pointing guns or shooting at animals when in natural areas. Unless the animal is a state listed animal in season, and you have the right hunting license, do not shoot at it. If you are alleging self-defense, you better have some very compelling facts, arguments and preferably witnesses that explain the need to use deadly force against an animal. South Carolina law protects virtually every wild (non-game) bird that you will encounter anywhere in the state. Most birds from eagles, falcons, owls and buzzards to cardinals, bluebirds, sparrows and finches are protected. The exceptions are the game birds that are subject to licensed hunting seasons like turkeys, doves, pheasants and some ducks. However, make sure that you know how to identify these birds before shooting at them and make sure that you have a license and are in the right hunting season. As a final note, the English Sparrow, Pigeon and Starling are considered feral and damaging. These birds are not protected by South Carolina Law (Section 50-1-30(2)) and you can shoot them if otherwise safe and lawful to discharge a firearm under the circumstances. Again, be sure to properly identify the bird before shooting because birds aren't just flying targets.

State Farmer's Markets

Section 5-190(D)(19) of the South Carolina Code of Regulations reads, "possession of firearms or fireworks is strictly prohibited on market properties, unless permitted in accordance with State law." Therefore, do not enter these properties with firearms unless you are carrying under a CWP. The language, *unless permitted in accordance with State law* also appears to mean those with exceptions like law enforcement or those with special permission from the presiding officer of the State Farmers Markets or the South Carolina Commissioner of Agriculture.

There are currently three State Farmers Markets in South Carolina. These are:

- Columbia State Farmers Market located at the: Southeastern Regional Market Terminal, 1001 Bluff Road in Columbia; the,

- Greenville State Farmers Market located at: 1354 Rutherford Road in Greenville; and the,

- Pee Dee State Farmers Market located at: 2513 West Lucas Street in Florence.

Pepper Spray

You may carry a spray can of pepper spray or other commercially available chemical irritant as described more fully in the *Tear Gas* section of this book. Tear gas type chemical irritants are specifically excepted from the criminal definition of poisonous gases in 16-8-10(13)(b) of the South Carolina Code of Laws if the device used to carry the irritant on or about the person is designed to carry no more than 50cc of irritant. You do not need a concealed weapons permit to carry a chemical irritant like pepper spray either openly visible or concealed (South Carolina Code of Laws Section 23-31-215(O)(2)).

Statutory Carry Exceptions

Again, the general rule is that it is illegal to carry a handgun, concealed or open. This rule is expressed in the first sentence of Section 16-23-20 of the South Carolina Code of Laws. A concealed weapons permit allows you to overcome this general prohibition in many situations if the handgun fits the definition of a concealable weapon. As mentioned earlier in this chapter, the South Carolina statutes create a laundry list of specific exceptions to the rule against carrying a handgun. We have already discussed some of the more pertinent exceptions but we will lay out the entire statutory list below. Some of the exceptions might seem redundant after reading the first part of this chapter but we thought it valuable to go through the entire list.

With or without a permit, you can carry a handgun under the following circumstances if you:

- are a regular salaried law enforcement officer, or a reserve police officer of a state agency, municipality, or county of the state or if you are an uncompensated Governor's constable, law enforcement officer of the federal government or other states when you are carrying out official duties while in the state (only federal government or out-of-state officers must be furthering official duties), South Carolina Code of Laws Section 16-23-20(1);

- are a deputy enforcement officer of the Natural Resources Enforcement Division of the Department of Natural Resources or a retired commissioned law enforcement officer employed as a private detective or private investigator, South Carolina Code of Laws Section 16-23-20(1);

- are a member of the Armed Forces of the United States, the National Guard, organized reserves, or the state militia **when on duty**, South Carolina Code of Laws Section 16-23-20(2);

- are a coroner or deputy coroner, **while engaged in official duties of his or her office**. A Coroner or deputy coroner is considered engaged in official duties when going to, or returning from, the actual performance of his duties. However, coroners and deputy coroners must be certified and trained by the South Carolina Law Enforcement Division (SLED) in the proper use of handguns. (South Carolina Code of Laws Section 17-5-110);

- are a special investigator appointed by the solicitor of the 3rd judicial circuit, **when on duty** (South Carolina Code of Laws Section 1-7-533);

- are a member of, or are the invited guest of, an organization authorized by law to purchase or receive firearms from the United States or the State of South Carolina or are a member of, or an invited guest of, a club organized for the purpose of target shooting or collecting modern and antique firearms **while you are at, or going to or from,** the place of target shooting or shows or exhibits, South Carolina Code of Laws Section 16-23-20(3);

- are a licensed hunter or fisherman who is **engaged in** hunting or fishing or are **going directly to or from** your place of hunting or fishing in a vehicle or on foot. *Directly* does not include stopping for gas or coffee or any other diversion, South Carolina Code of Laws Section 16-23-20(4);

- are a person regularly engaged in the business of manufacturing, repairing, repossessing, or dealing firearms, or if you are the agent of such a person. This is applicable as long as you are *carrying out the regular course of your firearm business*, South Carolina Code of Laws Section 16-23-20(5);

- are a guard authorized by law to possess a handgun and are *engaged in* protecting the property of the United States or an agency of the United States, South Carolina Code of Laws Section 16-23-20(6);

- are a member of an authorized military or civil organization while *parading or going to or from* your meetings, South Carolina Code of Laws Section 16-23-20(7);

- are in your home or on your real property, or if you have the permission of the owner or person in legal control of the real property, or if you are on property which you are in legal possession of or over which you have legal control, South Carolina Code of Laws Section 16-23-20(8);

- are in your vehicle and the handgun is secured in a closed glove compartment, a closed console, or in the trunk. You may also transport the handgun if it is in a closed container secured by an integral fastener and if that container is in the luggage compartment. It is legal to open the glove compartment, console, or trunk in order to retrieve a driver's license, registration, or proof of insurance in the presence of a law enforcement officer, South Carolina Code of Laws Section 16-23-20(9)(a);

- are carrying the handgun unloaded in a secure wrapper *from the place of purchase to your home or fixed place of business*. It is also allowed in the same manner if you are in the *process of moving* your residence or place of business, South Carolina Code of Laws Section 16-23-20(10);

- are a prison guard and you are *engaged in your official duties*, South Carolina Code of Laws Section 16-23-20(11);

- have a permit to carry from the State Law Enforcement Division as long as you are doing so under the conditions specified with regard to permits, (Concealed Weapons Permit included), South Carolina Code of Laws Section 16-23-20(12);

- are the owner, person in legal possession of, or person in legal control of a fixed place of business or if you are an employee of such a business. (This provision does not apply for employees if the business is a place that sells liquor, beer, or wine for on premises consumption. Again, see the Carry at Work Chart in the CWP chapter for an handy reference of the rules for carrying a handgun at work), South Carolina Code of Laws Section 16-23-20(13);

- are a person *engaged in* firearms related activities *while on* the premises of a fixed place of business, which conducts as a regular course of business, activities related to the sale, repair, pawn, or use of firearms, or firearms training, unless the premises is posted with a sign limiting the possession of firearms to holders of permits, South Carolina Code of Laws Section 16-23-20(14);

- are *transferring* a handgun directly to or from a vehicle to a location specified in this section as a place where you can legally possess the handgun, South Carolina Code of Laws Section 16-23-20(15);

- are *on* a motorcycle and you have the handgun secured in a closed saddlebag or other similar closed accessory container attached, whether permanently or temporarily, to the motorcycle, South Carolina Code of Laws Section 16-23-20(16).

Maybe you have noticed a theme regarding the words and phrases that are in bold italics. All of these emphasized words and phrases describe attributes like "while on duty," or "while going to and from," or "transferring." You must ensure that you understand these distinctions. If you have a concealed weapons permit, the rules are much more in your favor. If you do not, though, and you want to possess or transport a handgun, you are well advised to understand this list of exceptions. Failing to understand these distinctions might put you in danger of committing a crime under this statute without even knowing what you did wrong.

Law Enforcement Officer as a Party to a Civil or Criminal Action

Police and all other law enforcement officers can generally carry a handgun into a courthouse and even courtrooms, concealed or not. There are two exceptions however. The first is the protocol that the judge is the king of the courtroom. A judge can make it a rule in his or her courtroom that officers cannot have handguns.

Second, law enforcement officers are prohibited from carrying concealed weapons into a courthouse when they are a party to a civil or criminal action. This generally arises when an officer is a party in a divorce or domestic action. Family Court proceedings can strain emotions and it appears this prohibition is designed to prevent tragically violent reactions to sensitive testimony or unfavorable court decisions.

Mailing Guns

You cannot send a handgun through the regular mail. If you need to send a handgun, you must use a commercial carrier such as the type that has overnight and next day services. If you need to send a handgun through one of these commercial carriers, you must declare that the package contains a handgun and you must make sure it is unloaded and securely encased.

You can send rifles by U.S. Mail. However, you must declare it as a gun and make sure it is unloaded and securely encased. Unless you are a federally licensed firearms dealer, it is a violation of federal law to send a firearm by U.S. Mail or by any other carrier out of state unless you are sending it for repair or are returning it to a federal licensee.

Minimum Age for Possession of Guns

You must be at least 18 years of age to purchase, own or possess a handgun in South Carolina. If you are 18 years of age or older, state law allows you to purchase a handgun from a private seller (including private individuals selling at gun shows). However, federal law still requires that a person must be at least 21 year of age to purchase handguns or handgun ammunition from retailers or anyone else selling pursuant to a Federal Firearms License (including FFL licensees selling pursuant to their license at gun shows). Remember again that you must be at least 21 years of age to obtain a South Carolina CWP.

Section 16-23-30(3) of the South Carolina Code allows youths under the age of 18 to temporarily possess handguns for instruction under the immediate supervision of a parent or adult instructor. It is clear that the intent of this section is that the parent or adult instructor is right there with the youth as the parent or adult supervisor instructs the youth on handling or operating the handgun. The parent or instructor should not loan the handgun to a youth unless the parent or adult instructor is certain that the youth will have immediate supervision the entire time that the handgun is in possession of the youth. It should also be noted that this section allows for those under 18 years of age in the Armed Forces of the United States, active or reserve, National Guard, State Militia, or R. O. T. C., to possess handguns when on duty or training.

Youths under the age of 18 years of age are also subject to restrictions under Federal Law. 18 U.S.C 922(X) provides that it shall be unlawful for anyone under 18 years of age to possess a handgun or handgun ammunition. Be aware that the law also makes it unlawful for someone to sell, loan, give or otherwise provide a handgun or handgun ammunition to a person that is under 18 years of age. There are important exceptions to this general rule however. The first exception allows the *temporary transfer* of possession to someone under 18 years of age if the handgun and ammunition are possessed and used by the juvenile:

(i) in the course of employment, in the course of ranching or farming related to activities at the residence of the juvenile (or on property used for ranching or farming at which the juvenile, with the permission of the property owner or lessee, is performing activities related to the operation of the farm or ranch), target practice, hunting, or a course of instruction in the safe and lawful use of a handgun;

(ii) with the prior written consent of the juvenile's parent or guardian who is not prohibited by Federal, State, or local law from possessing a firearm, except—

(I)   during transportation by the juvenile of an unloaded handgun in a locked container directly from the place of transfer to a place at which an activity described in clause (i) is to take place and transportation by the juvenile of that handgun, unloaded and in a locked container, directly from the place at which such an activity took place to the transferor; or

(II)   with respect to ranching or farming activities as described in clause (i) above, a juvenile may possess and use a handgun or ammunition with the prior written approval of the juvenile's parent or legal guardian and at the direction of an adult who is not prohibited by Federal, State or local law from possessing a firearm;

(iii) the juvenile has the prior written consent in the juvenile's possession at all times when a handgun is in the possession of the juvenile; and

(iv) in accordance with State and local law;

The three other important exceptions allow for:

- a juvenile who is a member of the Armed Forces of the United States or the National Guard who possesses or is armed with a handgun in the line of duty;

- a transfer by inheritance of title (but not possession) of a handgun or ammunition to a juvenile; or

- the possession of a handgun or ammunition by a juvenile taken in defense of the juvenile or other persons against an intruder into the residence of the juvenile or a residence in which the juvenile is an invited guest.

There is no minimum age for possession of rifles and shotguns. (Remember that FFL dealers can only sell rifles and shotguns to purchasers 18 years or older). When it comes to possessing rifles and shotguns, South Carolina law makes no requirement for supervision of minors by adults. However, be mindful of South Carolina hunting laws regulating hunting by persons under 18 years old.

Train Children about Guns

What is your philosophy regarding children and your guns? You should research methods of training children about guns and employ a training program for children who might possibly come in contact with your guns. The chapter on gun crimes and liability discusses this topic further.

Conclusion

It is essential that you know the rules for transporting or carrying a weapon with or without a permit. Again, always be aware of where your gun is at all times. You must always assess the legality of your gun's location. Having a concealed weapons permit will allow you to transport and carry your gun in many situations where it is otherwise illegal.

Summary Points

- Always be aware of the location of your guns.

- The general rule is you can't carry a concealed weapon without a permit.

- You can carry a concealed weapon under certain circumstances even without a permit.

- You can carry non-lethal weapons like pepper spray even without a permit.

- If eligible, get your concealed weapons permit right away.

Chapter 6
Weapon Crimes and Lawsuits

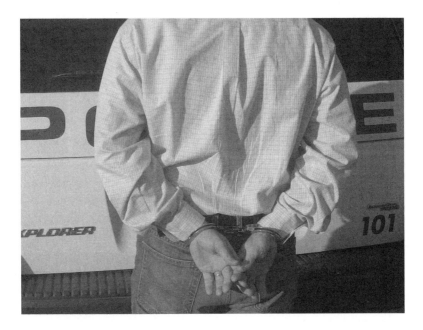

Gun owners possess an incredibly powerful but also dangerous instrumentality. You hold a tool to protect your family, your country and yourself but it comes with a huge responsibility. The law punishes people who harm others with dangerous instrumentalities like guns. This chapter is designed to help you avoid having criminal charges and avoid getting sued as a result of your gun.

Criminal Law versus Civil Liability

Guns can get you into trouble in both the criminal and civil realms of the law. Criminal liability generally comes when an individual intends to harm another. It can also come when someone does something so reckless or negligent that there is a reasonable expectation someone will get harmed.

A criminal case is usually the State versus the person accused of the harm. The state of South Carolina prosecutes criminal cases through its state attorneys. To find an accused guilty of a crime the State has the heavy burden of proving guilt beyond any reasonable doubt. Wrongdoers are held accountable through forfeiture of guns, jail time, fines, probationary sentences, and restitution. In general, a felony is a high level crime with a possible sentence of more than one year in jail. Similarly, a misdemeanor is a lower level crime with a possible sentence of less than one year in jail. However, this is not always the case. For instance, a violation of Section 16-23-465 of the South Carolina Code of Laws is a misdemeanor with a 3 year jail time and a lifetime federal firearms disability. Be aware also that some crimes are state misdemeanors with the potential penalty of greater than 2 years in jail that subject convicts to a federal firearms disability.

Civil law deals with non-criminal wrongs (although some criminal statutes provide for civil penalties). Generally, this is where an individual harms others through negligence. Negligence is acting in a manner that falls below the standard of care that a reasonable person would have used under the same circumstances. Civil law also has other theories of liability in addition to negligence.

While a civil court of equity has a broad array of tools to remedy wrongs, the main tool of the civil courts is money judgments. Private parties and their attorneys generally handle both sides of a civil dispute. Civil cases are proven by the lesser standard of preponderance of the evidence which simply means that the winner is the side that is more believable.

In a nutshell, crimes are a violation of written statutes that carry a penalty of gun confiscation, jail time, a fine, probation and payment of restitution to the victim. Civil wrongs are wrongs by people against other people that are not classified as crimes. The penalties for civil wrongs are money damages or an equitable remedy like an order to stop doing something or to specifically do something.

Let's take a closer look at how guns can get you into trouble both criminally and civilly. We'll start with the crimes and then discuss civil liability. For the sake of brevity, we will assume that you know crimes like murder and armed robbery. Usually, these crimes take a considerable amount of evil aforethought. Instead, we will identify some less obvious crimes that, none-the-less, carry serious criminal liability.

Reminder about the Lifetime Federal Firearms Disability

Before we get started though, a quick reminder about the lifetime federal firearms disability. As you go over the following crimes, pay attention to the potential penalty for a conviction or adjudication. Many of the crimes carry a sufficient potential penalty to saddle you with a lifetime federal firearms disability. This disability is explained more fully in the chapter on *Legal Disability and Executive Clemency*. With that important note out of the way, let's get back to the crimes that you must avoid.

Pointing a Gun at Someone

Never point a gun at someone unless in legitimate self-defense. Pointing a loaded, or even unloaded, gun at someone is a crime. Did you read that? It is a crime to point even an *unloaded* gun at another person. Under South Carolina Section 16-23-410, pointing a gun at someone is a felony that is punishable by a fine at the discretion of the court and up to 5 years in jail. With that potential penalty, this offense also carries the penalty of a lifetime federal firearms disability. This section does not apply to theatrical or like performances.

If you have to point a gun in legitimate self-defense, the criminal and civil courts will allow you a legal defense. We devote an entire chapter of this book to legal self-defense with a firearm so please refer to that Chapter for a more thorough discussion. To keep it simple for now, it is a crime to point a loaded or unloaded gun at someone except for in legitimate self-defense.

Entering the Residence of Others while Armed

As mentioned in the concealed weapon chapter, even permit holders may not carry a concealed weapon into the residence or dwelling of another person without the express consent of the owner or tenant. Obviously this is true for those without a permit. This crime is a misdemeanor and can be punished by a fine of not less than $1,000 or up to one year in jail or both. Further, if you have a permit, it will be revoked for 5 years.

Criminal Negligence

Section 16-3-60 of the South Carolina Code of Laws defines criminal negligence as the reckless disregard of the safety of others. Recklessness involves a very high degree of negligence where a person's actions show callous indifference toward others. Under this section, the definition is only used in conjunction with involuntary manslaughter which means the killing of another without malice. In the context of guns, examples might include shooting in an unsafe direction. For instance, some geniuses think that a 4th of July celebration is not complete without firing guns into the sky. If a bullet returns down and kills someone (which has happened), the shooter has committed involuntary manslaughter. Involuntary manslaughter is a felony with the penalty of not more than 5 years in prison. It also brings a lifetime federal firearms disability.

Discharging a Gun into a Dwelling, Building or Vehicle

Under Section 16-23-440 of the South Carolina Code of Laws, it is unlawful to discharge a firearm at or into a dwelling, other building, structure, or enclosure, which is regularly occupied by people. It is also unlawful to discharge a firearm at or into a vehicle, aircraft, watercraft, or other conveyance, device, or equipment while it is occupied. This crime is very similar to reckless endangerment and you can be simultaneously charged for both. The penalty is up to a $1,000 fine or up to 10 years imprisonment or both and a lifetime federal firearms disability.

Taking a Law Enforcement Officer's Weapon

Under Section 16-23-415 of the South Carolina Code of Laws, it is unlawful to take a firearm, stun gun, or taser device from the person of a law enforcement officer or a corrections officer. Violation of this section is a felony with a penalty of not more than 5 years of jail time or a fine of not more than $5,000, or both and a lifetime federal firearms disability. Additionally, taking it will almost certainly require you to engage in battery on a law enforcement officer which is a separate crime.

While you might think that you would never take a weapon from a law enforcement officer, it is possible that you could find yourself in a situation where you might get mixed-up with a law enforcement officer. This can happen either by mistake or because the officer is out of control and unlawfully posing an imminent risk of death or serious bodily injury to you or someone else.

First, let's look at some circumstances where you might get mixed up with a police officer. For simplicity sake, try to categorize law enforcement officers as either: uniformed and on-duty, plain clothed and on-duty, or plain clothed and off-duty.

The simplest scenario is if the officer is uniformed and on-duty. Attempting to take a firearm, stun gun, or taser away from a uniformed law enforcement officer is a felony. If you actually are able to take it away, you have likewise committed a felony.

If the officer is on-duty but is not in uniform, it gets a little tricky. Under these circumstances, you must know, or have a reason to think, that the person is a police officer and that he is on-duty. The court will judge your thought process by the "reasonable man" standard. This means that a court will try to objectively determine what a reasonable person would think under the same circumstances. In simple terms, would the average guy have thought that the person in plain clothes was a police officer and that he was on-duty at the time that you tried to take his weapon.

Here are two examples that demonstrate the two opposite ends of the knowledge spectrum:

Not Guilty - You are walking on the street and you turn the corner and see a guy with a gun stuck into a woman's back. She has her hands up. You sneak up on the guy and are able to snatch his gun away from him. He is a plain clothes on-duty policeman.

You took his weapon but a court might find that a reasonable person under the same circumstances would not have thought that the man was a law enforcement officer. One possibility is that you thought that the man was robbing the woman.

Maybe Not Guilty – Same scenario except that you notice that the man is pulling handcuffs from his back pocket. Police usually carry handcuffs so there is some reason for you to believe that he is a police officer.

Probably Guilty - Same scenario except that you notice that the man has a badge clipped to his belt and is pulling handcuffs from his back pocket. Now you have two reasons to think that the man is a police officer. He is getting handcuffs and a reasonable person would think that the badge signifies a police officer.

Guilty – Same scenario except that you notice that the man also has a uniformed policeman standing right next to him. A reasonable person would not think that a uniformed police officer would stand idly by while a criminal sticks a gun in the woman's back.

South Carolina law does not prohibit off-duty law enforcement officers from carrying either open or concealed weapons. Officers don't even have to have a concealed weapons permit to carry concealed while in their street clothes. However, officers are under the policy of their individual department. In other words, each law enforcement office can institute its own policy about officers carrying guns while not on duty. It is not a criminal offense for the officer to not follow his or her office's policy but it might be cause for employment action like a suspension or termination. It seems very unlikely that any law enforcement administrator would restrict his or her officers from carrying a weapon under most circumstances. Therefore, it is a reasonable assumption that law enforcement officers are always carrying a weapon.

In any of the above circumstances, if the law enforcement officer gives you consent to take his or her weapon, there is no crime. It is probably very rare to have a law enforcement officer give you consent to take his or her weapon. However, situations might arise where consent is conceivable. For instance, an officer could be wrestling with a suspect and yell for you to take his or her taser to subdue the suspect. Probably does not happen much but it is possible.

Secondly, while highly unlikely, it is conceivable that you encounter an out of control law enforcement officer who unlawfully attacks you or someone around you with an imminent threat of death or serious bodily injury. If you determine that you are or someone around you is under an imminent threat of death or serious bodily injury from an out of control officer, you have the right to use deadly force to defend yourself or others. Your actions will be judged on the reasonable man standard discussed in the self-defense chapter.

Guns at School

(For a more thorough discussion about guns on school grounds, make sure that you have read the Rules for Schools section in the *Possessing and Transporting Guns without a Permit* chapter.)

You cannot bring a firearm to any school grounds in South Carolina. Under Section 16-23-420 of the South Carolina Code of Laws, it is a crime to possess a firearm of any kind on any property owned, operated, or controlled by a private or public preschool, elementary, middle or high school, college, university, technical college, or post secondary institution without the *express* permission from the school authorities. Express permission can be written or verbal. While not an explicit requirement, the best practice is to get permission in writing on school stationary and signed by the authorized school officer (a detailed discussion of authorized school officers can be found in the chapter on *Possessing and Transporting Guns without a Permit*).

If you do not have express permission, possessing a firearm at any school is a felony punishable by a fine of up to $5,000 or imprisonment for up to 5 years or both under Section 16-23-420. Section 16-23-430 provides for an additional or separate felony for bringing a deadly weapon unto elementary or secondary school grounds. The penalty under Section 16-23-430 is a fine of up to $1,000, a jail term not to exceed 5 years, or both and you may also have your weapon confiscated if convicted or adjudicated. In addition to firearms, you can be charged for possession of knives with a blade over two inches long, blackjacks, metal pipes, metal poles, or any other type of object that can be legitimately deemed a weapon at an elementary or secondary (middle and high) school under Section 16-23-430. Both of these sections subject the convicted or adjudicated to a lifetime federal firearms disability.

There is an exception for guards, law enforcement officers, members of the armed forces, and students of military science. There is another exception for married students who reside in apartments provided by the school and who have the permission of the persons who are responsible for security at the school. Again, do not consider anything less than a document with the authentic signature of a school authority as sufficient permission.

The prohibition of weapons on school grounds does not apply to the roads through the schools. Be careful though because you must not stray from the roads open to the public and maintained by the state or local government and which are open full-time to the public. Generally, you can possess weapons on the big streets that get you through campus 24 hours a day. If you pull onto a small private road owned by the school or a parking lot, you are risking criminal liability.

The school prohibition is not limited to a main school campus because areas like ball fields, off-campus parking, auxiliary structures and any other school property likewise triggers the prohibition. Additionally, be aware that weapons are prohibited from school events that are held off of school property. Therefore, weapons are prohibited on school sponsored activities like field trips, off-campus sporting events and community service projects.

In summary, you cannot possess a firearm on any school grounds or at any event connected with a school. This applies to colleges, technical schools, public and private elementary, middle and high schools, and all of the special schools. Possessing a firearm at a school or school function, regardless of having a concealed weapons permit, is a serious crime.

Public Buildings

With or without a Concealed Weapons Permit, it is unlawful under 16-23-420 of the South Carolina Code of Laws to possess a firearm in any publicly owned building. This Statute has been discussed above in the *Guns at School* section so refer to that section for information on penalties. For non-school properties, this is generally interpreted to mean inside a building and not simply on the premises. For example, you can legally possess a firearm in the glove box of your vehicle in the parking lot of a public building but you cannot bring the same firearm into the building. An important exception exists, however, for interstate highway rest areas. Concealed Weapons Permit licensees are authorized to carry concealable weapons, concealed into interstate highway rest areas and possess them inside the rest areas.

No Firearms on the Capitol Grounds

Again, with or without a permit, Section 10-11-320 of the South Carolina Code of Laws makes it unlawful to discharge, carry, or otherwise have a firearm readily accessible while on the capitol grounds or within the capitol building. For a more detailed including the partial exception for CWP holders, see the *Can I Carry on the Capitol Grounds* section in the *Possessing and Transporting Guns without a Permit* chapter.

Trap Guns

Under Section 16-23-450 of the South Carolina Code of Laws it is unlawful to construct, set or place a loaded trap gun, spring gun, or any other similar device. A trap gun is a device, which might or might not include an actual gun, which is designed to be triggered by movement such as someone opening a door. As an example, people might consider constructing a trap gun mechanism to shoot or scare home invaders.

Merely constructing a trap gun is a misdemeanor punishable by up to a $500 fine and between 30 and 365 days in jail or both. If the trap goes off and someone is killed, you will probably be charged with murder. Even if the trap gun just goes off on someone, but does not kill that person, you might still be facing attempted murder.

You will discover later that the law never permits you to protect property with deadly force. The idea behind a trap gun is to protect property from an invader when the property owner is not around. Therefore, it is never a good idea to construct a trap gun. Find other ways to secure your property and leave the trap guns to Wile E. Coyote and the Roadrunner.

Forfeiture of Weapon if Crime involves Concealed Weapons

Under Section 16-23-460 of the South Carolina Code of Laws, carrying a concealed weapon of the type usually used for the infliction of personal injury is a misdemeanor and the potential penalty is from $200 to $500 with a potential jail term of between 30 and 90 days. This section also provides that the weapon must be *forfeited* to the county or municipality. If you are convicted under this section, you will lose that weapon forever. So, you should assume that all concealable weapons (defined in the *Concealed Weapons Permit* chapter) and handguns are included in this definition of concealed weapon.

You must realize that this statute works alone or can be tacked-on to many other crimes if a concealed weapon was being carried during the commission of the crime. Violation of this section can be tacked-on to both violent and non-violent criminal offenses. This section does not prohibit you from carrying a concealed weapon pursuant to a CWP or any statutory exception that allows concealed carry. This also does not apply to rifles, shotguns, dirks, slingshots, metal knuckles, or razors; unless they are used with intent to commit a crime.

Additional Penalty for Firearms in Business that Sell Alcohol

As mentioned previously in this book, under Section 16-23-465 there is an increased penalty for illegally carrying a firearm into a business which sells liquor, beer, or wine for consumption on the premises. This crime is a misdemeanor with the penalty of a fine of up to $2,000 or jail for up to 3 years or both. Because the potential jail term for this state misdemeanor is over 2 years, conviction or adjudication under this statute will burden the convict with a lifetime federal firearms disability. See the *Concealed Weapons Permit* chapter for a full discussion of carrying a firearm into a business that sells alcoholic beverages for onsite consumption.

Drinking and Shooting

Under South Carolina Code of Laws Chapter 23-31-400(B), it is unlawful to use a firearm if you are under the influence of alcohol or a controlled substance. Violations are a misdemeanor and may be punished with a fine of up to $2,000 or imprisonment for up to 2 years or both. There is an exception if you are required to use the firearm lawfully in self-defense.

If you are shooting and someone thinks you are drunk, the observers can call the police. If the investigating officer arrives and has a reasonable suspicion that you have been using drugs or drinking too much, you will be given a blood test or urine test or both to determine if you are in fact under the influence. If you refuse to submit to the test, that fact can and will be used against you in the criminal proceeding. However, while the results of any blood or urine test will be used in a criminal prosecution for using the firearms under the influence, the results cannot be used in a criminal prosecution for possession of the controlled substance.

If you are arrested for using a firearm while under the influence but the arresting officer does not request a blood or urine test, you can request such testing. If you know you have not consumed alcohol or used drugs, it is a good idea to get tested right there. If you do request the testing and the officer refuses to give you the tests, you cannot be prosecuted.

If used at trial, the results of the blood or urine test used at trial create certain legal presumptions. If the test reveals that you have .05% or less alcohol in your blood, it is presumed that you were not under the influence of alcohol at the time of the test. If the test reveals that there is greater than .05% but less than .08% alcohol in your blood, no inference is created either way (under or not under the influence). Finally, if the test reveals that you had .08% or greater alcohol in your blood, a presumption is created that you were under the influence at the time of the test.

These presumptions are only a starting point. It is still possible to show by other evidence that you were under the influence even though you had .05% or less blood alcohol level. The jury can consider other evidence like slurred speech or stumbling. There are also field sobriety tests which might indicate intoxication. It is also possible to have .08% or greater blood alcohol level and not be found under the influence. A jury decides if you were under the influence or not but you should never put yourself in that position.

This statute should not cause you to hesitate before using a gun in self-defense just because you had been consuming alcohol or were required to use prescription drugs. It is basically designed to prevent the purposeful use of firearms under the influence of alcohol or drugs for reasons other than self-defense. There are certainly circumstances that could arise where a person is drinking alcohol or under the influence of controlled substances and is confronted with a deadly threat that requires the defensive use of deadly force.

Possessing a Firearm while Unlawfully Dealing in Alcohol

It is unlawful under Section 61-6-4180 to possess a firearm or weapon while unlawfully dealing in alcohol. Under this section, if a person unlawfully manufactures, transports, or sells alcoholic liquors or aids or assists in any manner in one or more of these acts and at the time of the unlawful manufacturing, transporting, selling, aiding, or assisting has on or about his person or has on or in a vehicle which he uses to aid him in any such purpose or in his actual or constructive possession a firearm or weapon of like kind, he is guilty of a misdemeanor and, upon conviction, must be imprisoned not less than 1 year nor more than 3 years, or be fined not less than $500 nor more than $1,500. The three year potential sentence of this state misdemeanor means that a conviction also brings a lifetime federal firearms disability. If the firearm is concealed while this statute is violated, the additional possible penalty is a $200 to $500 fine, jail time between 30 and 90 days, and forfeiture of the firearm.

Discharging a Firearm within 50 yards of a Public Road while Drunk

South Carolina Code of Laws Section 16-17-530(c) provides that any person who shall, while under the influence, or feigning [faking] to be under the influence, of intoxicating liquor, without just cause or excuse, discharge any gun, pistol or other firearm while upon or within fifty yards of any public road or highway, except upon his own premises, shall be deemed guilty of a misdemeanor. Upon conviction, the penalty is a fine of not more than $100 or jail time of not more than 30 days.

This Statute seems like it would appear in a wacky laws book. While it is dealing with the serious topic of firearms, it is so odd that it deserves a second look. In plain English, the law basically says, "Unless you have a very good reason to do so, or you are on your own premises, it is against the law to shoot a gun within 50 yards of a public road if you have been drinking or if you are faking that you were drinking." It is already illegal to shoot a gun while under the influence of alcohol except for in lawful self-defense, so why this additional charge? Also, is a bullet any less dangerous from 51 yards as opposed to 50 yards? Also, why would someone pretend to be drink while shooting a gun? Or why would anybody be pretending to be drunk anytime. For the legislature to deem this law necessary, it can only mean that somewhere; somehow; sometime in the past . . . somebody got hurt and some nut tried to use the excuse that he was only pretending to be drunk when he shot his gun within 50 years of a public road.

Allowing Mental Patients and Mental Prisoners Access to Firearms

It is a felony to provide a firearm to mental patients or mental prisoners. Section 44-23-1080 of the South Carolina Code of Laws provides that it is unlawful for anyone to willfully or even negligently provide mental patients or prisoners access to firearms. The fine is not less than $1,000 and not more than $10,000 and the jail time is not less than one year and not more than ten years. If the judge wants to, he or she can give you both the fine and the time. Also, because this is a felony, conviction or adjudication brings a lifetime federal firearms disability. Further, on top of these stiff criminal penalties, you might also get hit with a civil lawsuit. So, never provide a mental patient or prisoner even a chance to access your firearms.

Providing Prisoners with Firearms

Section 24-3-950 of the South Carolina Code of Laws makes it a felony criminal offense to furnish or attempt to furnish a prisoner under the jurisdiction of the Department of Corrections with contraband. *Any and all firearms* are defined as contraband in South Carolina Code of Regulations Chapter 33-1. It is likewise a felony for the prisoner to possess a firearm under this statute. The penalty is a fine of not less than $1,000 nor more than $10,000 or imprisonment for not less than one year or more than ten years, or both. Of course, you become subject to the lifetime federal firearms disability also.

Similarly, Section 24-7-155 makes it a felony for any person to furnish or attempt to furnish any prisoner in any county or municipal jail, prison, work camp or overnight lockup facility with contraband [a firearm] as defined in South Carolina Code of Regulations Chapter 33-1. The penalty is a fine of not less than $1,000 nor more than $10,000 or imprisonment for not less than one year nor more than ten years, or both. You can also add on the lifetime federal firearms disability.

If you are currently an inmate, Section 24-13-440 of the South Carolina Code of Laws makes it unlawful for an inmate of a state correctional facility, city or county jail, or public works of a county to carry on his person a dirk, slingshot, metal knuckles, razor, firearm, or any other deadly weapon, homemade or otherwise, which usually is used for the infliction of personal injury upon another person, or to willfully conceal any weapon within any Department of Corrections facility or other place of confinement. An inmate violating this section is guilty of a felony and, upon conviction, must be imprisoned not more than 10 years. A sentence imposed under this section must be served consecutively to any other sentence the inmate is serving.

Don't forget about South Carolina Section 16-23-460. Again, that section tacks on an additional misdemeanor for carrying a deadly weapon usually used for the infliction of personal injury concealed about his person. The charge is a misdemeanor with a fine of not less than $200 nor more than $500 or imprisonment not less than thirty days or more than ninety days. But the kicker is that the firearm must be forfeited also.

Criminally Negligent use of a Firearm before, during or after Hunting

Under Section 50-1-85(3) of the South Carolina Code of Laws, it is unlawful for any person to use a firearm or archery tackle in a criminally negligent manner while in preparation for, engaged in the act of, or returning from hunting. Criminal negligence is defined as the reckless disregard for the safety of others. A conviction under this section is a misdemeanor with four possible penalties depending upon the nature of the criminal negligence. Upon conviction:

(1) in a case where no personal injury or property damage occurs, a fine of not more than $200 or jail for not more than 30 days;

(2) in the case of property damage only, a fine of not more than $1,000 nor less than $500 or jail for not more than six months, and the court must order restitution to the owner of the property;

(3) in the case of bodily injury to another, a fine not less than $500 nor more than $2,500 or imprisoned for not more than 2 years; if the bodily injury results in disfigurement, total or partial permanent disability, you can be imprisoned for not less than 60 days nor more than 2 years;

(4) in the case of death, you can be imprisoned for not less than 3 months nor more than 3 years. (Violation of this subsection also brings a lifetime federal firearms disability because the potential sentence for this state misdemeanor is greater than 2 years.)

These are mandatory sentences so no part of the minimum fines and penalties provided in this section may be suspended by any Court in South Carolina.

In addition to the criminal penalties under this section, the South Carolina Department of Parks, Recreation and Tourism (SCDPRT) must immediately seize any hunting license of a person charged under this section and, upon conviction, the hunting privileges of the person convicted under item (1) or (2) will be suspended for 1 year. A person convicted under item (3) will lose his privilege to hunt for 3 years, and a person convicted under item (4) will lose the privilege of hunting for 5 years.

If the person is convicted under this section and then decides to hunt while his license is suspended under the provisions of this section, he must be fined not less than $500 nor more than $2,500 or imprisoned for not more than 2 years and shall have his hunting privileges suspended for an additional 5 years. The person may not obtain another hunting license until he has satisfactorily completed a hunter's safety program conducted by the SCDPRT.

Discharging a Firearm at a Boat Ramp or Landing

For some reason, boat ramps can really bring out the worst in people. Maybe the confrontation starts because someone's kid on a personal water crafts put a big rubber streak against someone's hot new graphics. Maybe it starts because some family decides to wash their boat on the ramp while there is a line of boats waiting to put into the water. Or, maybe it starts because some yahoo didn't take a picture of the bass before he threw it back into the water. For whatever reason, boat ramps breed confrontation. Just an opinion, but fresh water ramps usually have more testosteroned-up hotheads than do salt water ramps. Either way, under South Carolina Code of Laws Section 50-21-146, it is unlawful to discharge a firearm at a boat landing or ramp. A person who discharges a firearm at a public boat landing or ramp is guilty of a misdemeanor and, upon conviction, must be fined between $25 and $200 or imprisoned for between 10 days and 30 days. This is in addition to other crimes that may apply. Some have suggested that this discussion about boat ramps might be better placed under the *Drinking and Shooting* section! Needless to say, if alcohol is involved there might be additional crimes tacked-on.

Teaching, Demonstrating, or Making a Firearm for Civil Disorder

Under Section 16-8-20 of the South Carolina Code of Laws, it is a felony to:

- teach or demonstrate to another person the use, application, or making of a firearm or destructive device which is capable of causing injury or death if the person knows, has reason to know, or intends that what is taught or demonstrated, will be employed unlawfully for use in, or in furtherance of, a civil disorder; or

- assemble with one or more persons for the purpose of training, practicing, or instructing in the use of a firearm or destructive device which is capable of causing injury or death to persons if the training, practice, or instruction is used in furtherance of an unlawful purpose or a civil disorder.

Upon conviction for a first offense, the convict must be fined not more than $5,000 or imprisoned for not more than 5 years, or both. Upon conviction for a second or subsequent offense, the convict must be fined not more than $10,000 or imprisoned for not more than 10 years, or both. Because these are felonies, a conviction or adjudication under this section will also bring a lifetime federal firearms disability.

This section has some exceptions. Nothing in the section prohibits:

- an act of a law enforcement officer performed within his official capacity;

- training for law enforcement officers conducted by or for an agency or a political subdivision of a state or an agency of the United States;

- activities of the National Guard or of the armed forces of the United States; or

- classes intended to teach the safe handling of legal firearms for hunting, recreation, competition, or self-defense.

Increased Penalty for using Concealed Weapon in Violent Crimes

If you are convicted of assault, assault and battery, assault or assault and battery with intent to kill or manslaughter and it appears at your trial that the assault, assault and battery, assault or assault and battery with intent to kill or manslaughter was committed with a concealed firearm, South Carolina Code of Laws Section 16-3-610 provides for an increased penalty. The section requires the presiding judge to, in addition to the punishment for the underlying crimes, add the increased penalty of additional incarceration time of not less than 3 months and not more than 12 months, with or without hard labor, or a fine of not less than $200. The judge has the discretion to give either the jail time or the fine or both. Because either the underlying crime is a felony, or the increased penalty causes the combined potential jail time to exceed 2 years for the underlying state misdemeanor, conviction under this section also subjects the convict to a lifetime federal firearms disability.

Additionally, Section 16-23-490 provides for an increased penalty for possession of a firearm during commission of, or attempt to commit, a violent crime. If a person is in possession of a firearm, or visibly displays what appears to be a firearm, during the commission of a violent crime and is convicted of committing or attempting to commit a violent crime as defined in Section 16-1-60 of the South Carolina Code of Laws, the penalty is a mandatory 5 years in jail without parole or "good-time" in addition to the punishment provided for the principal crime. Again, because either the underlying crime is a felony, or the increased penalty causes the combined potential jail time to exceed 2 years for the underlying state misdemeanor, conviction under this section also subjects the convict to a lifetime federal firearms disability.

Tear Gas and Chemical Irritant Weapons

Except for authorized law enforcement officers, Section 16-23-470 of the South Carolina Code of Laws makes it is unlawful to possess, use, transport, buy, or sell a tear-gas machine or a tear-gas gun if the projectile can or does contain greater than 50 cubic centimeters of tear gas. It is also unlawful to possess, use, transport, buy, or sell any parts, ammunition, shells, or equipment that may be used in a tear-gas machine or a tear-gas gun with a cartridge of over 50 cubic centimeters. A violation of the section is a misdemeanor and is punishable by up to a $5,000 fine and up to 3 years in jail. Uh-oh: a potential sentence of up to three years in jail? Here is another example of a state misdemeanor with a potential jail sentence of more than 2 years so the possibility of a lifetime federal firearms disability is, pardon the pun, triggered.

The statute does a poor job of defining tear gas because traditional *tear gas*, Mace, and pepper spray are distinct chemicals from on another. None of these compounds are gasses. However, they are all probably coved under this prohibition. What is commonly called *tear gas* is either orthochlorobenzalmalononitrile or chloroacetophenone, known respectively as CS and CN. These are the most common compounds used by law enforcement for riot control and other applications. Civilians can get their hands on CS and CN also. Dibenz(b,f)-1,4-oxazepin, abbreviated to CR, is another compound commonly called *tear gas* and used by law enforcement. At normal temperatures and standard atmospheric pressure, these compounds are not gasses but rather white crystals. To disperse the compound, the crystals must be put into a solvent and aerosolized. Mace is a trade name for another CN crystalline compound that must be put into a liquid and aerosolized. Pepper spray is oleoresin capsicum (OC) extracted from chili peppers. OC is a dark orange, oily liquid, which must be put into a liquid and aerosolized.

Without any better definition of tear gas from the statute, the best practice is to assume that any of the above compounds are defined as tear gas for the purpose of the prohibition.

Section 16-23-470 allows possession or use of a tear-gas machine or tear-gas gun if it is used only for self-defense and not capable of firing a shell with a capacity of more than 50 cubic centimeters of tear-gas. Some new items on the market maybe fit this exception. Manufacturers have created paint ball sized pepper spray (OC) balls for use with paintball guns and shotgun shells that fire pepper spray (OC) projectiles. So long as the projectile contains less than 50 cubic centimeters of pepper spray, these projectiles appear legal under the self-defense exception. Remember, however, that the gun and tear gas must only be possessed or used for self-defense.

Objects Designed to Cause Damage by Fire or Detonation

Section 16-23-480 makes it unlawful to manufacture or possess any object which is designed to cause damage by fire, ignition, or detonation. Here is another statute section that uses very broad and vague language such as: *any object which is designed to cause damage by fire*, so it is open for unintended interpretations. A torch can be used by a roofer to melt the tar on roof laps for better sealing, or a torch can be used by an arsonist to burn down buildings. So, should a person be prosecuted for possession of a torch as the existing overly-broad statute would allow, or should a person only be prosecuted for the misuse of the torch? You can probably think of items that are designed to cause damage by fire, ignition or detonation. In any case, manufacturing or possessing such an object is a felony punishable by a fine and up to 5 years in jail. This felony also subjects the convicted or adjudicated to a lifetime federal firearms disability. Although typical retail fireworks use fire, they are designed for entertainment and not to cause damage by the fire or ignition. Therefore, it is unlikely that anyone would be prosecuted for using retail fireworks under this statute. You never know though.

Transfer of Handguns to Convicts, Minors & Mentally Incompetents

South Carolina Code of Laws Section 16-23-30(A)(1) makes it unlawful to sell, offer to sell, deliver, lease, rent, barter, exchange, or transport for sale any handgun to any person who has been convicted of a crime of violence in any court in the United States, the several states, commonwealths, territories, possessions, or the District of Columbia. It is also unlawful to sell, deliver, lease, barter, exchange or transport for sale any handgun to any person who is a member of any subversive organization, is a fugitive from justice, is a habitual drunkard, is a drug addict, or who has been adjudicated mentally incompetent under Section 16-23-30(A)(2). Similarly, it is against the law to sell, deliver, lease, rent, barter, exchange, or transport for sale any handgun to any person who is under the age of eighteen (18) years old under Section 16-23-30(A)(3). This does not apply to the issue of handguns going to members of the armed services, the National Guard, the state militia, or the ROTC when on duty or training or temporarily for instruction and under the supervision of the instructor.

Also, under Section 16-23-30(A)(4) it is unlawful to sell, offer to sell, deliver, lease, rent, barter, exchange, or transport for sale any handgun to any person who has been adjudicated unfit to carry or posses a firearm by a circuit court judge. Such adjudication will have been made after a law enforcement officer, prosecuting officer, or the court itself initiated an action on the fitness of an individual. A person can only be determined unfit after the opportunity for notice and hearing.

All of the crimes under 16-23-30 are felonies. A person, including a dealer, who violates these statutory sections, upon conviction, must be fined not more than $2,000 or imprisoned not more than 5 years, or both under Section 16-23-50(A)(1). Additionally, the handgun involved must be forfeited under Section 16-23-50(B).

151

Because it is a felony, a convicted or adjudicated person is subject to a lifetime federal firearms disability.

What if I Find a Gun?

South Carolina Code of Laws Section 16-23-55 sets forth a procedure for returning a found handgun in the *Offenses Involving Handguns* Chapter (23). This section does not require turning over a found handgun to law enforcement nor does it create any penalties for not doing so. Presumably, the procedure is included in the *Offenses Involving Handguns* Chapter to help law enforcement and prosecutors recover discarded or lost handguns that were involved in crimes. The incentive is that the finder can own the gun "free and clear" from any claims of ownership in a little more than 90 days after turning it over to law enforcement. Law enforcement must make a diligent inquiry to determine the true owner of the handgun and determine whether the handgun was stolen or involved in a crime. Law enforcement must also advertise in the area newspaper that the gun has been found. If the handgun is not claimed within 90 days of the first publication in the newspaper, the finder can apply for the handgun but must also pay all advertising and other costs incidental to returning the handgun.

The applicant must be a resident of South Carolina, however, residency is not required of a person who is on active duty in the United States military and who is in possession of a current United States military identification card. The application is the same as if purchasing a handgun from a dealer. In other words, the applicant must complete the same purchase forms and go though the National Instant Criminal Background Check System (NICS) as if the applicant is buying a handgun from a local gun shop or any other federal firearms licensee. Incidentally, the NICS is mandated by the Brady Handgun Violence Prevention Act (Brady Act) of 1993, Public Law 103-159. The Act has done nothing to curb handgun violence by criminals and has only made it more difficult and expensive for law abiding citizens to exercise their right to keep and bear arms.

Machine Guns, Military and Sawed-Off Weapons

In common terms, it is unlawful for you to have anything to do with a machine gun or firearm commonly known as a machine gun, military firearm, sawed off shotgun, or sawed off rifle. Under South Carolina Code of Laws Section 16-23-220, 230 and 240 you are prohibited from possessing, buying, selling storing, transporting, renting, giving away, or just about anything that pertains to these weapons. If convicted, you could be fined up to $10,000 and jailed for up to 10 years or both. Conviction or adjudication also brings a lifetime federal firearms disability.

There are exceptions that allow you to legally possess these types of weapons. However, a detailed discussion of the exceptions is beyond the scope of this book. If you are interested in legally possessing these weapons, machine gun dealers are generally knowledgeable of the requirements.

One exception is for military personnel, law enforcement personnel and private citizens who have complied with the strict provisions of the National Firearms Act (NFA). The NFA has license and tax/fee provisions that are beyond the scope of this book so, again, consult an attorney before possessing these types of weapons. Another exception is for weapons that are rendered harmless and not usable and are kept only for display as relics. Further, antique firearms are also exempted. Finally, there is a way that you can legally acquire these types of weapons through inheritance.

Acquiring Machine Guns or NFA Restricted Guns through Inheritance

You can either give or receive an NFA restricted firearm through a properly drafted will or trust. An important consideration is whether the firearm is transferred from the decedent or settlor to the ultimate recipient as an individual or in the name of a partnership, company, association, trust, estate, or corporation. In either case, you must first file an application in duplicate and pay the ATF $200 as a registration tax.

If you apply for registration as an individual, you must obtain the signature of a Chief Law Enforcement Officer, provide two photographs, and provide two sets of fingerprints. The Chief Law Enforcement Officer can be the Chief of Police, the Sheriff, head of the State Police, a District Attorney or State Attorney, or any other person that is acceptable to the Director of ATF. Applying for registration in the name of a corporation or a trust is easier and does not require the signature of the Chief Law Enforcement Officer.

There are advantages and disadvantages to each of these methods of registration and a full discussion is beyond the scope of this book. To determine which is best for you, find an attorney with knowledge of both firearms and estate planning.

Barrel Length under the NFA

To remain outside of the NFA prohibitions, rifles barrels must be at least 16 inches. Shotguns barrels must be at least 18 inches long. To measure the barrel length of a gun, place a wood or plastic rod into the barrel with the action closed. Then mark the rod and pull it back out of the barrel and measure from the mark to the end of the rod. The distance from the mark to the end of the rod is the length of the barrel. In addition to the restrictions on barrel length, the overall length of the rifle or shotgun must be at least 26 inches.

Military-Type Accessories under the NFA

A machine gun is defined as a firearm that can shoot more than one shot with a single pull of the trigger. So called "hell fire" mechanisms make semi-automatic guns shoot like a machine gun. The hell fire device rapidly pulls the trigger after each preceding shot. Hell fire devices do not render your semi-automatic illegal because your weapon is not made a machine gun with one. Be warned, however, that the ATF has ruled Akins Accelerators in violation of the NFA.

It is also illegal to own parts which can be used to convert a gun into a machine gun. Illegal parts might include frames or receivers of machine guns and also any combination of parts which can be assembled to make a machine gun.

Further, it is a crime to own a silencer, an undersized firearm, a cane gun, unhinged pen guns which fire tear gas through use of a self contained cartridge, and any pistol which is fitted for a shoulder stock. As before, you can be around these weapons if you have a license under the NFA.

The most important thing that you must know about these weapons is to stay away from them unless you thoroughly understand the NFA. If you want to do anything with these weapons, put down this book for now and go see a knowledgeable machine gun dealer, find a current book on machine gun law or schedule an appointment with an attorney knowledgeable with machine gun law. Federal laws regarding these weapons are detailed and the penalties are stiff.

Possession of a Firearm by those Convicted of Certain Crimes

Under Section 16-23-30(B) of the South Carolina Code of Laws, it is a felony for any person convicted of certain crimes of violence to own or possess a handgun. This is true even if the conviction originated in another state.

Crimes of violence are defined in South Carolina Code of Laws Section 16-23-10 as: murder, manslaughter (except negligent manslaughter arising out of traffic accidents), rape, mayhem, kidnapping, burglary, robbery, housebreaking, assault with intent to kill, commit rape, or rob, assault with a dangerous weapon, or assault with intent to commit any offense punishable by imprisonment for more than one year. Note that conviction is defined not only as a jury verdict of guilty but also *adjudication of guilt* through pleas of guilty, pleas of nolo contendere, and forfeiture of bail. A person, including a dealer, who violates Section 16-23-30(B), upon conviction, must be fined not more than $2,000 or imprisoned not more than 5 years, or both under Section 16-23-50(A)(1). Additionally, the handgun involved must be forfeited under Section 16-23-50(B).

One or more of the crimes of violence described above might not be designated as a felony but are state misdemeanors punishable by more than 2 years in jail. So, even if the actual sentence or punishment was less, the fact that the state misdemeanor has the ***potential*** punishment of more than 2 in jail renders the convict ineligible to possess a firearm. Please see *Appendix I* for more information on federal firearms disability that results from a conviction of most federal and state felonies, federal misdemeanors with a potential jail term of more than 1 year, or state misdemeanors with a potential jail term of more than 2 years.

Armor Piercing Bullets

It is illegal to manufacture, sell, or deliver armor piercing ammunition to anyone other than law enforcement personnel. Armor piercing ammunition has a truncated cone and a core made of steel or another material of equal hardness. In 1994, the federal law added any ammunition with a full metal jacket if that jacket is more than 25% of the total weight of the bullet. If you buy ammunition from a reputable gun shop, you will never run into armor piercing ammunition. As to owning or possessing armor piercing ammunition, it is not technically illegal to own or possess armor piercing bullets unless you load them into a handgun or if you have the intent to commit a crime with the rounds.

It is also unlawful to use, transport, manufacture, possess, purchase, or sell any ammunition or shells which are coated with polytetraflouroethylene (Teflon). Ammunition coated with Teflon is considered armor piercing. A violation here is a felony punishable by a fine of up to $5,000 and jail for up to 5 years. A violation will also subject the convicted to a lifetime federal firearms disability.

Illegal to Provide Guns to Illegal Aliens

In addition to any federal law, South Carolina Code of Laws Section 16-23-530 makes it illegal to knowingly sell, offer to sell, deliver, lease, rent, barter, exchange, or transport for sale into South Carolina a firearm to a person knowing that such person is not lawfully present in the United States. A violation of this section is a misdemeanor with a penalty of up to $2,000 fine, 3 years in jail or both. Because this is a state misdemeanor with a potential jail term of more than 2 years, a violation also subjects you to a lifetime federal firearms disability.

Just to make things fair, it is also illegal for the illegal alien to possess, purchase, offer to purchase, sell, lease, rent, barter, exchange, or transport into South Carolina a firearm. So, in addition to any other law the illegal alien is violating for being in the United States, this section provides for felony liability with a fine of not more than $10,000, imprisonment for not more than 10 years, or both. Because it is a felony, the violator is also subject to a lifetime federal firearms disability. But, if the person is an illegal alien, he or she probably doesn't give a hill of

157

beans about any of these laws anyway so the prospect of a lifetime federal firearms disability is not much of a deterrent.

Possessing Stolen Handguns

Under South Carolina Code of Laws Section 16-23-30(C), it is a felony to knowingly buy, sell, transport, pawn, receive, or possess any stolen handgun. Under Section 16-23-50(A)(1), the penalty for a violation is a $2,000 fine, up to 5 years in jail, or both. Additionally, the handgun must be confiscated under 16-23-50(B). Don't forget to also add a lifetime federal firearms disability because this crime is a felony.

Possessing Handguns with Altered Serial Numbers

Under South Carolina Code of Laws Section 16-23-30(C), it is also a felony to knowingly buy, sell, transport, pawn, receive, or possess any handgun from which the original serial number has been removed or obliterated. Again, under Section 16-23-50(A)(1), the penalty for a violation is a $2,000 fine, up to 5 years in jail, or both. Additionally, the handgun must be confiscated under 16-23-50(B). You can also add on a lifetime federal firearms disability because this crime is a felony.

Shooting at Trains

South Carolina statute 58-17-4100 prohibits the willful shooting of firearms at a train. The prohibition applies to all portions of a train, not just cars typically occupied by people, and it does not matter if the train is moving or not. It seems that this law was required because some people think it is either fun or challenging to hit trains with bullets. The penalty is not more than $500 fine or 5 years in jail. This is a felony crime that will leave the convicted person with all of the troubles of a felony record and lifetime federal firearms disability. The person who shoots at a train might also be charged with other crimes if applicable. If the cars are occupied or someone is hurt or killed, even more charges will pile on. Do not point your muzzle at trains or anything else that you do not intend to kill or destroy.

Legal Defense to a Crime

You never want to get in the position of breaking the law and getting arrested or charged. However, there are legal defenses if you are arrested or charged. Say, for instance, that you are legally carrying your gun and forget it's there when you try to enter the gate area of an airport, or a courthouse or some other prohibited place. The fact that you actually forgot about the gun is a legal defense. Lack of knowledge is a legal defense.

Another legal defense is using your weapon for lawful self-defense. The lawful use of self-defense is a worthy of an entire chapter so the *Self-Defense* chapter will more fully discuss your right to defend yourself.

Civil Lawsuit Liability

Civil liability arises when someone is wronged in a manner that does not violate a criminal law or is in conjunction with a criminal wrong. A civil wrong can subject you to a money judgment. Some established bases for a civil lawsuit include: negligence, negligent entrustment of a dangerous instrumentality, assault, trespass, trespass to chattels, infliction of emotional distress, and nuisance. This list is not exhaustive. A court can use its inherent power to hear almost any dispute. But, for the purpose of this book, we will look at the abovementioned causes of action.

Negligence is conduct that falls below the conduct of a reasonable person under the same circumstances. It is important to understand that the standard is not subjective. This means that you are not judged on whether you think that your actions are reasonable.

Instead, your actions are judged against what others think a reasonable person would do under the same circumstances. Therefore, it is wise to add a measure of caution regarding the handling and storing of your firearm because others might not think that your actions are reasonable.

Negligent entrustment of a dangerous instrumentality arises if you entrust your weapon to someone that you know, *or should know*, has a propensity to do purposeful or negligent wrongful acts. The person you entrust (lend) the weapon to can be an adult or a minor, competent or incompetent. So, be very selective about who you entrust your firearms with, if anyone.

Assault is placing another in imminent fear of an immediate harm. The idea is that the first person makes a second person fear that the second person will immediately be harmed by the first person. Again, the reasonable person standard is applied.

In the context of guns, assault can occur if a person simply brandishes a firearm. Under some circumstances, a person might reasonably fear harm from a firearm even when the person with the firearm had no intention to cause the fear. Facing civil liability for assault, you should never brandish or expose a firearm unless you are sure that no one around you will be placed in immediate fear as a result.

Trespass is an unauthorized entry upon the property of another. Be aware that sending an object like a bullet upon the property of another is a trespass. You do not have to intend to commit a trespass to be liable. Instead, you must only intend to go upon the property of another. Therefore, you can still be liable if you did not intend to commit a trespass but you intentionally went on another's property (this is a somewhat confusing concept that lawyers and judges have come up with). You are permitted to trespass in the event of an emergency or for self-defense.

Civil liability for trespass can accompany the criminal liability mentioned earlier in this chapter. For instance, you can be held criminally liable for entering a business with a concealed weapon when that business has posted a "No Concealable Weapons Allowed" sign. You can also be sued for money damages by the same business owner for the trespass.

Trespass to chattels is damaging or destroying the property of another. With respect to guns, liability arises when an errant shot destroys the property of another. Animals are considered property under the law. Therefore, if you accidentally damage another's building, vehicle, or pet, you can be sued for money damages.

You can be held civilly liable for intentional or even negligent infliction of emotional distress upon another. You must be aware that, under the right circumstances, a jury could find that your firearm caused another emotional distress. Your conduct must be extreme and outrageous, but, none-the-less, you can be held civilly liable for inflicting serious emotional pain upon someone.

Nuisance involves denying another the quiet enjoyment of their property. You can create civil liability for nuisance by creating noise or smoke with your gun. Also note that, while a nuisance cannot also be a trespass, a trespass can be a nuisance.

A Note about Keeping Guns Away from Children

A special note should be made about keeping guns away from children. The courts recognize that children are not simply "little adults" but rather immature people who are not as mentally developed as most reasonable adults. Children are not able to assess risk like adults can. Similarly, children cannot foresee the consequences of actions as most adults can.

You might have seen television programs where parents are shown hidden camera video of their children finding a gun. To the parents' horror, some of the children handled the planted guns and even pointed them at other children in the room.

In some circumstances, parents can be held liable for the actions of their children even when an adult is not around. Further, adults directly supervising children can be held liable for the consequences that result from that adult's negligence. For these reasons, adults must have a strategy for safely keeping guns around children. Maybe your strategy can be to combine a gun safe with an educational program like the NRA's *Eddie Eagle: Stop! Don't Touch, Leave the Area and Tell an Adult* program. Maybe you have one loaded pistol with a small fingerpad gun safe next to your dresser and the rest of your guns unloaded in a safe. The authors are not making recommendations here but emphasizing the point that you must have some reasonable strategy for balancing the defensive safety of a firearm against the potential that a child can cause unintended harm.

Fortunately, there are many good products that prevent unauthorized or accidental access to guns. The most effective mechanism is called, not surprisingly, a gun safe. A finger pad gun safe can be placed in a nightstand and uses an electronic fingerboard that opens immediately with a pin number. Also, there are trigger locks and bolt locks for guns that would not be needed for a threat. Finally, guns can be kept in places where children do not go like relative's homes or gun club lockers.

Will my Insurance Cover Me if I get Sued or Arrested?

Homeowner's insurance and business liability insurance policies generally have a personal liability provision. Many people also have "umbrella" liability policies that supplement and increase liability coverage. In general, these policies provide liability indemnification for occurrences at the home or business, in or about a vehicle, or even anywhere else in public. These policies insure against the *negligent* acts of the insured but not the intentional acts of the insured. So, as you read through this civil liability section, keep in mind that you will not be covered if the act is considered intentional.

If you are sued for negligence, and the negligence is a covered occurrence in your policy, the insurance company will provide you with an attorney and defend the lawsuit. The policy will also pay if it is determined that another was injured as a result of your negligence. If you are arrested for a crime, liability policies will not cover you so the insurance company will not provide you with a defense attorney. There are, however, legal service insurance plans that provide you with an attorney if you are arrested or need other routine legal services. Those policies generally only cover the legal fees of defense but will not indemnify you against claims or judgments. See the *Self-Defense* Chapter for more discussion of insurance liability policies.

Summary Points

- A firearm opens many opportunities for both criminal and civil liability.

- Never point a gun at someone except in lawful self-defense.

- Never have a gun on school grounds without permission.

- Do not go near machine guns or shortened barrel guns without fully understanding the requirements of the National Firearms Act.

- Never set a trap gun.

- If you have been convicted of certain crimes or have other legal disabilities without executive clemency, you cannot possess firearms.

- Some forms of ammunition are illegal.

- Purchasing ammunition over the counter at your local gun shop or from a reputable website is a simple way to increase the probability that the ammunition is legal.

- Do not tamper with a gun's serial number or buy a gun with an altered serial number.

Chapter 7
Self-Defense

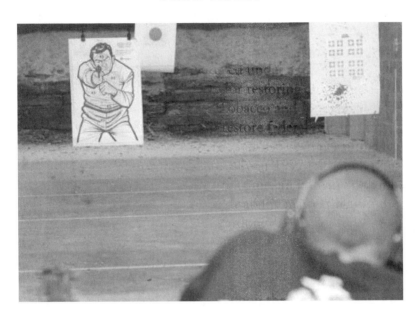

Introduction

You should always look to avoid confrontation and dangerous situations. If there are traditionally dangerous parts of your town, keep yourself and your loved ones away. Drive an extra few miles to avoid areas that have high concentrations of crime. Further, be familiar with your surroundings. Military trainers emphasize *situational awareness* which is the discipline of staying alert to your surroundings and consciously discerning the safety risk at all times. Your alert mind is your first line of self-defense.

No matter how hard you try to avoid bad people, though, a deadly situation can materialize at any time and in any place. This chapter will deal with lawful self-defense. Self-defense is an affirmative legal defense for actions that would otherwise be criminal. You have a

right to inflict force upon others if you are legitimately defending
yourself or others.

Under South Carolina law, if a person is charged with a crime,
and subsequently claims self-defense, the burden is upon the prosecution
to disprove beyond a reasonable doubt at least one of the elements of
self-defense. If the prosecution can not do so, then the claim of self-
defense must stand and the criminal charge is defeated.

Please read this chapter thoroughly because it is important that
you know the law of self-defense. You should view this chapter as a
whole and not as separate sections because some sections interact with
other sections. If any chapter deserves to be read over and over, this is
the chapter. (Author's note: for a real-life case study of the law of self-
defense in South Carolina, you should read the trial record of Jason
Dickey posted on the GrassRoots GunRights South Carolina website.
The record contains the entire trial testimony that reads as easy as a
paperback novel and is similarly riveting. The case shows how critical yet
unreliable the *reasonable person standard* can be. Read it and see if you
agree with the 12 jurors who found that Jason Dickey acted
unreasonably.)

The Unfortunate Context of Self-Defense

It is unfortunate that our society has come to the point where
honest and peaceful, law-abiding citizens have to carry guns during their
normal daily activities. Guns are fascinating, "cool," and often
beautifully built machines but they are primarily designed to cause
serious damage to whatever their ammunition hits. Guns can be heavy,
bulky, and can get clothes or purses greasy if not cleaned correctly. Also,
guns cause stress because the carrier must be mindful of where the
muzzle is pointed, keeping fingers off of the trigger, the legality of
possession and concealment, and preventing the gun from escaping into
the hands of untrained children or unauthorized users. Carrying a gun

consistently adds complexity to daily life. Even so, more and more people are carrying guns to defend against a deadly attack.

That being said, the criminals and crazy nuts generally have the advantage because they are not worried about the legality of using their weapon. In a survival situation, law-abiding citizens might hesitate because of uncertainty about the law of self-defense. Fear of criminal prosecution or a lawsuit can cause the *paralysis of analysis*.

The best way to overcome the paralysis of analysis is to read this chapter over and over and to imagine self-defense scenarios in your mind as you go through your day. Think of scenarios that you often find yourself in. For instance, the next time that you are in a parking lot at night, think of how you would react if you come upon a group of armed thugs. Would you react differently if the threat is moving fast or slow or if any of the thugs have a knife as opposed to a gun? At what point would you consider the thugs' actions a deadly attack? At what point would you pull-out your gun from its holster and shoot at the attackers? What could you do or would you do if other people are around? As another example, think of how you would react if you and your coworkers were held hostage by some armed robbers. If you have an opportunity to shoot the robbers while their backs are turned, is it legal to do so? Another example is to envision shopping in a crowded mall when some crazed gunman starts shooting with a rifle. Would it be legal to shoot back? Would it be more beneficial to find a good hiding place first or start firing back first? Think through the scenarios and then try to find the best answers in this book. We say *best* answers because most of the time there is no *right* answer but only the best answer given the circumstances and our legal system.

Another way is to have a few very simple rules. For instance, the only time that the general public should know that you are carrying a gun, or see your gun, is when you are using it to defend against a deadly attack. At best, brandishing a weapon will get you into criminal liability or defeat your claim of self-defense. At worst, brandishing your gun will prevent you from effectively defeating the deadly threat. Owning the element of surprise is one way to overcome the built-in advantage that criminals have. Further, brandishing a weapon is generally an ineffective deterrent to someone who is really out to victimize you. So, have simple rules like: never pull your gun out unless you intend to use it to shoot at a legitimate deadly attack against you or someone you are protecting. We give you a few other simple rules in this chapter.

We expect that the people reading this book are law-abiding citizens who do not want to shoot somebody. Law abiding citizens carrying guns for self-defense are not a problem. It is the criminals and people with untreated mental conditions that are a problem. That being said, if you come into the predicament where you are required to use your gun, and you misjudge the situation, you might end up prosecuted, seriously injured or dead. None of these alternatives are welcome but they do happen.

On balance, the most important thing is that you have the ability to defend against a deadly attack. The justice system must be respected but you should not let it intimidate you from legally carrying your gun and using it if you have to. In the unfortunate context of defending your life with a gun, there are no great options. In the end, protecting your life, or the life of some other innocent person, is more important than anything else.

Distinction between Deadly and Non-Deadly Force

You must have a sound understanding of the difference between deadly force and non-deadly force. Deadly force is defined as force that is likely to cause death or great bodily harm. Clearly, any gun has the ability to cause death or great bodily harm. Similarly, a sharp knife and swinging a baseball bat have the ability to cause death or serious bodily harm. An automobile steered directly at another can cause death or serious bodily harm. Even the bare hands of a strong person can cause death or serious bodily harm to a weaker, more vulnerable or surprised person.

Alternatively, non-deadly force is force that is not likely to cause death or serious bodily harm. Spraying pepper spray is not likely to cause death or serious bodily harm. Similarly, the bare hands of a weak person are not likely to cause death or serious bodily harm.

If you are starting to realize that the differences between deadly and non-deadly force are not black and white, you are beginning to understand the concept. If the use of deadly force comes before a court of law, all facts relating to the incident will be carefully scrutinized.

The Four Elements of Self-Defense in South Carolina

Under common law in South Carolina, four elements must exist:

- You must be without fault in bringing-on the violent encounter between you and the other person(s);

- You must actually believe that you are in imminent danger of loss of life or serious bodily injury or you must actually be in such danger;

- You must use deadly force only if a reasonable or prudent man of ordinary firmness and courage would have believed himself to be in imminent danger of loss of life or serious bodily harm or, if you actually were in such danger, the circumstances were such to warrant a man of ordinary prudence, firmness and courage to use deadly force against the other person(s);

- Unless you are in a place that you are lawfully entitled to be, you had no other probable means of avoiding the danger of losing your own life or sustaining serious bodily injury than to act as you did in the particular instance.

The next sections look at these elements one-by-one.

Without Fault

In order to raise self-defense, you cannot be the aggressor or primogenitor of the violent encounter. Simply put, you cannot be the one who started the whole thing that resulted in a violent encounter. Further, you are prohibited from doing anything to escalate an encounter. The law requires that you be *without fault,* not that you simply are less at fault than the other guy. Did you catch that? You must be without fault throughout the entire encounter with the other person. Make sure you understand the concept of being without fault throughout the entire encounter.

Say that you are driving on I-26 and there is a jerk going slow in the left lane. Next to that guy is an SUV in the slow lane going the same speed as the jerk in front of you, thereby creating a rolling blockade. Your irritation builds with every passing mile. Irritation turns to anger and you start to tailgate the left lane loafer. After a few miles of tailgating, the loafer motions you to pull over for a closer encounter of the violent kind. You pull over and argue and then the loafer comes at you with some type of deadly attack. Under these facts, you will probably not gain the legal defense of self-defense because you are not without fault in bringing about the violent encounter. There is a good chance that you would be charged and that a jury could find that somewhere in those events you had some level of fault in either continuing or escalating the episode.

Alternatively, say that you are on I-26 near Newberry at 1:00am and you get a flat tire. You pull over to repair the tire and you have your concealed weapon with you. Some opportunistic criminals see you in a vulnerable position and stop to "help." As they help you with the tire, one of the guys comes at you with a knife or gun. You pull out your weapon and shoot the attackers in self-defense. Under this simple fact pattern, you did not bring on the attack and you did nothing throughout the episode to escalate the attack. Therefore, you would probably not get charged. Even if you did get charged it is likely that a jury would find that you satisfy the "without fault" element of legal self-defense.

Belief of Imminent Threat of Death or Serious Bodily Harm

You can only use deadly force in self-defense if the threat to you is imminent. Imminent means that you are under an immediate threat. In other words, someone is posing a bona fide threat of death or serious bodily harm to you right there at that location and at that time. Put another way, the threat must be right before both physically and in time.

As to the physical aspect of this element, the important factor is that the weapon presented against you must be capable of causing harm based upon the distance between you and the threat. A knife is a deadly weapon but it must be used in close range and by a person with the physical ability to use the knife. Pistols and shotguns are deadly weapons but they have deadly ranges that are generally less than rifles. A car can be a deadly weapon if it is traveling in the right direction and within a certain distance of a victim.

As to the timing aspect of this element, the important factor is that the attack occur immediately prior to, or contemporaneously with, your self-defense reaction. So, the time prong is not satisfied if someone calls you on the phone and says that he or she is going to come over and kill you. It is also not satisfied if someone creates a deadly attack towards you and you get away and then you go back and shoot the person. The threat must either directly proceed or happen contemporaneously with your self-defense actions.

171

The main point here is that, under a self-defense claim, juries will be asked to determine if the deadly object, if any, combined with the nature and circumstances of the attack, was right before you, right then and right there. We will next show a few simple examples that illustrate the self-defense element of *imminent threat*.

Assume that your spouse or romantic interest and you are out on a movie date and you get a phone call from your date's obsessively jealous or crazy ex. The ex begins to say that your date is bad for you and that, "if the ex cannot have her or him, nobody can." The ex says that he or she is going to go to your house later that night and kill you. Hearing that news, you become scared because you know that the ex is a violent person, is bigger than you, and has been previously convicted of assault with a deadly weapon. To protect yourself, you drive over to the ex's house and shoot and kill the ex. Under these circumstances, it is very likely that you will be charged with murder and found guilty by a jury. The ex's threat was not imminent because the ex was talking with you over the phone and said that he or she would not kill you until later.

Now let's assume that the ex did not call you but rather surprised you by meeting both you and your date outside of the theater. From a short distance away, the ex begins to approach you in a very aggressive posture and pulls out a knife and says that he or she is going to kill you. You are honestly in fear for your date's life and your own. At that point, you pull out your concealed weapon and shoot him so that he is rendered immobile. Under these facts, you might get arrested but a jury has ample evidence to find that the threat was imminent. If you did get arrested, hopefully the prosecutor would see that you acted in legal self-defense and drop any charges against you. If the worst scenario occurs and you go before a jury, the jury would have good evidence for an acquittal.

Again assume that the ex surprises you both outside of the theater. Let's change the facts a little to say that the ex has no history of violent behavior that you are aware of, is much smaller than you, and never gives any indication that he or she has a deadly weapon. While, "in your face," the ex tells you that he or she is going to get a gun out of the car and shoot you. You have no idea where the car is but you know that it is not close because there are no cars directly around where you are standing. Believing that the ex is going to go to his car and get a gun to shoot you, you pull out your gun and shoot the ex first. Even though the ex was saying that he or she was going to get a gun to kill you, and approached you in a somewhat threatening manner, you could be successfully charged with murder or manslaughter because there is weak evidence that the threat was imminent. In other words, the threat was not right before you, right then and right there.

The above scenario becomes more complicated if you do not shoot the ex then and there but, instead, stand your ground while the ex goes back to his or her car and returns with a gun. That type of scenario will be examined following the *Reasonable or Prudent Man Standard* element of self-defense. The next section will introduce you to the Protection of Persons and Property Act that provides a very important legal presumption that a threat is imminent under certain circumstances.

Imminent Threat Presumed in Home, Dwelling or Occupied Vehicle

To their great credit, the South Carolina Legislature passed, and on June 9, 2006, Governor Sanford signed, the Protection of Persons and Property Act (the Act). The main purpose of that legislation is to create statutory legitimization of the "Castle Doctrine." The bill also gives statutory protection to "stand your ground" in most legitimate defensive situations. The Castle Doctrine is a very old doctrine of law that recognizes the adage that a person's home is his castle. It also extends that adage to include a person's business and occupied vehicle.

For the purpose of this section, the relevant portions of the Act (Section 16-11-440 (edited) of the South Carolina Code of Laws) provide:

> A person is *presumed* (emphasis added) to have a reasonable fear of **imminent** peril of death or great bodily injury to himself or another person when using deadly force that is intended or likely to cause death or great bodily injury to another person if the person:
>
> (A) against whom the deadly force is used is in the process of unlawfully and forcefully entering, or has unlawfully and forcibly entered a dwelling, residence, or occupied vehicle, or if he removes or is attempting to remove another person against his will from the dwelling, residence, or occupied vehicle; and
>
> (B) who uses deadly force knows or has reason to believe that an unlawful and forcible entry or unlawful and forcible act is occurring or has occurred.

In plain English, this statutory section simply imputes you with a *legal presumption*. Legal presumptions are discussed later in this chapter. The legal presumption imputed to you is that the threat that you faced was imminent under the listed circumstances. Therefore, if you are required to use deadly force against another and those circumstances were in place, a jury trying you would be legally required to start with the presumption that the threat that you faced was imminent.

The Statute is very specific as to the places where the presumption will arise. The threat must take place at a dwelling, residence or occupied vehicle. The Statute defines *dwelling* as a building or conveyance of any kind, including an attached porch, whether the building or conveyance is temporary or permanent, mobile or immobile, which has a roof over it, including a tent, and is designed to be occupied by people lodging there at night. Conveyance here can mean anything from a million dollar rock star RV to a broken school bus attached to the side of a home. *Residence* is defined as a dwelling in which a person resides either temporarily or permanently or is visiting as an invited guest. Finally, *vehicle* means a conveyance of any kind, whether or not motorized, which is designed to transport people or property. This can be anything from an airplane to a car to a chartreuse microbus. There are also specifications regarding the nature of the attack such as the manner in which the intruder is entering the dwelling or vehicle.

The "Reasonable" or "Prudent Man" Standard

If you use deadly force to repel a deadly attack, you will be judged by the "reasonable man" standard. That is, if you are charged, the judge or jury will decide whether a reasonable person would have acted similarly under similar circumstances. Therefore, the facts surrounding the incident are very important. You are better served by facts that bolster the reasonableness of your use of force.

Consider this simplified example: you are approached by a person who points a gun at you and says that he or she is going to kill you. You have a concealed pistol. You draw your pistol and shoot the person. With these limited facts, your use of the pistol seems a reasonable use of deadly force. However, as we have already seen in the previous sections, additional facts can either bolster or diminish the *perceived* reasonableness of your response. If the encounter happened at night in a dark alley and the assailant demanded money and fired a shot towards you, those facts tend to bolster the perceived reasonableness of your response. Alternatively, the perceived reasonableness of your response is diminished if the encounter happened in daylight on a crowded street and an assailant wielded a bright orange toy pistol.

While your use of deadly force in any of the above scenarios might be perceived as reasonable, a jury could likewise perceive that they were not. The point here is that there is no clear line as to what facts make the use of deadly force reasonable. There are countless factual scenarios and judges and juries see things differently. Making things more difficult is the fact that a victim usually has only seconds to determine whether or not to respond with deadly force.

Reasonable Fear Presumed in Home, Dwelling or Occupied Vehicle

Similar to the statutory legal presumption of *imminent threat* discussed under the previous element of self-defense, the Act provides for a presumption of reasonable fear of a deadly attack under certain circumstances. For the purpose of this section, the relevant portions of the Act (Section 16-11-440 (edited) of the South Carolina Code of Laws) provide:

> A person is *presumed* (emphasis added) to have a **reasonable fear** of imminent peril of death or great bodily injury to himself or another person when using deadly force that is intended or likely to cause death or great bodily injury to another person if the person:
>
> (A) against whom the deadly force is used is in the process of unlawfully and forcefully entering, or has unlawfully and forcibly entered a dwelling, residence, or occupied vehicle, or if he removes or is attempting to remove another person against his will from the dwelling, residence, or occupied vehicle; and

(B) who uses deadly force knows or has reason to believe that an unlawful and forcible entry or unlawful and forcible act is occurring or has occurred.

As before, this statutory section simply imputes you with a legal presumption. The legal presumption imputed to you is that you had a reasonable fear of an imminent threat of death or serious bodily harm. If the threat arose under the listed circumstances, a jury trying you would be legally required to start with the presumption that you had a reasonable fear of an imminent threat of death or serious bodily harm to you or someone else. As before, the statute is very specific as to the places where the presumption will arise. The threat must take place at a dwelling, residence or occupied vehicle. There are also specifications regarding the nature of the attack such as manner in which the intruder is entering the dwelling or vehicle.

Legal Presumptions

Now is a good time to discuss legal presumptions in general. The first thing you need to know about presumptions is that they are starting points in the law. This means that if certain conditions are met, the jury is charged with drawing certain conclusions based upon those facts. Be aware though that these presumptions can be overcome by evidence to the contrary. For example, you are presumed to be in reasonable fear of imminent death or great bodily harm if you use deadly force to stop an attacker or invader who is in the process of unlawfully and forcefully entering, or has unlawfully and forcefully entered a dwelling, residence, or occupied vehicle. However, this presumption can be overcome if evidence is presented that you clearly were never in fear of an imminent attack by the intruder.

Maybe you knew for a fact that your frail neighbor had plans to break into your house unarmed, while you were not at home, to steal some of your 1883 Carson City Silver Dollars. When you encounter the neighbor in your house, you see no weapons on the neighbor and the neighbor immediately runs away from you to get away. At no time are you in fear of a deadly attack. Not wanting the neighbor to get away, you shoot the neighbor in the back or side or maybe even in the chest. If charged with a crime and you raise the defense of self-defense under these facts, you will be imputed with the presumption that you were in reasonable fear of an imminent deadly attack. However, the jury has ample facts to overcome the presumption and find your use of deadly force unjustified under the circumstances.

No Other Probable Means of Avoiding the Danger

Under South Carolina common law, the fourth element of a successful claim of self-defense is that you had no other probable means of avoiding the dangerous threat other than to use deadly force upon the attacker. In other words, you have a duty to retreat if you had a reasonable opportunity to do so. However, the Protection of Persons and Property Act has done away with this common law duty under most of the circumstances that you are likely to face.

For the purpose of this section, the relevant portion of the Act (Section 16-11-440 (edited) of the South Carolina Code of Laws) provides:

> (C) A person who is not engaged in an unlawful activity and who is attacked in another place where he has a right to be, including, but not limited to, his place of business, has no duty to retreat and has the right to stand his ground and meet force with force, including deadly force, if he reasonably believes it is necessary to prevent death or great bodily injury to himself or another person or to prevent the commission of a violent crime as defined in Section 16-1-60.

In plain English, this section of the statute eliminates the common law duty to retreat and allows you to stand your ground and apply deadly force to a deadly threat. However, there are certain conditions that must be met to overcome the common law duty to retreat. These conditions are:

- You cannot be engaged in illegal activity at the time of the episode;

- You must be in a place where you have a legal right to be;

- You must reasonably believe that deadly force is needed to prevent death to you or someone else or to prevent a violent crime as defined in Section 16-1-60 of the South Carolina Code of Laws.

Assuming that you are not engaged in illegal activities and that you are in a place where you have a legal right to be, these conditions are pretty broad and allow you to stand your ground in most situation that you find yourself in. Remember also though that you must reasonably believe that deadly force is needed to prevent death or a violent crime. Again, if you are in your home, dwelling or occupied vehicle, under the conditions discussed in the *imminent threat* and *reasonable or prudent man standard* sections, this presumption is imputed to you.

Remember under the *imminent threat* element discussed earlier in this chapter, we created a scenario where an ex surprises you and your date outside of a theater. Again, we changed the original facts to say that the ex has no history of violent behavior that you are aware of, is much smaller than you, and never gives any indication that he or she has a deadly weapon. While, "in your face," the ex tells you that he or she is going to get a weapon out of the car and come back and kill you. You have no idea where the car is but you know that it is not close because there are no cars directly around where you are standing.

Instead of shooting the ex right there as in a previous scenario, you allow the ex to go to his or her car. From the other side of the parking lot, you see the ex retrieve what appears to be a gun or large knife from the car. A good distance away, the ex continues to yell that he or she is going to kill you and starts walking quickly towards you from way across the parking lot. Again, you have a concealed weapon on you. Even though you have a pistol on you, you clearly know that you are far enough away that you could start running back to the theater to get to safety. Assuming that you are not doing anything illegal and that you have not been told to keep off the theater property by the owners, you have no duty to retreat and you can use deadly force against the man if the threat evolves to the point where you have a reasonable belief that the ex poses an imminent threat of death or serious bodily harm to you or your date. Remember though, because you are not in a home, dwelling, or occupied vehicle, the imminent threat and reasonable belief elements will not be automatically imputed to you.

Under the same scenario, let's alternately assume that you were at the theater with your date prior to a drug deal. Your plan was to meet some drug buyers after the movie in the theater parking lot. You have the drugs ready for sale on you and your buyers are in the parking lot. In that case, you are engaged in illegal activity when the episode started. Looking back at the facts, it is clear that you have a probable means of avoiding the danger with your retreat. Therefore, there is a good likelihood that you would have a duty to retreat under those facts.

In any scenario, you should seriously consider the practicality of a retreat over standing your ground. The best practice is to always avoid any potentially deadly encounter by getting away. If you have a chance to safely walk or run away from a problem, certainly do so. A humiliating retreat beats getting shot, an arrest, holding cells, bail, jail, attorney's fees and the risk of jury misinterpretation any day.

These fact patterns are simple examples to help you conceptualize the law. For all self-defense scenarios, the more facts that you have to support your actions, the stronger your self-defense claim. As you might see, the best practice is to have the proper self-defense mindset when carrying a weapon for self-defense. If you can safely avoid the danger, take that option every time. But, if you reasonably believe that you or someone else is in imminent danger of death or serious bodily injury, you have the right to protect yourself or others with deadly force.

More on the Protection of Persons and Property Act

There are some important exceptions to the Act that you must be aware of. First, the presumptions do not apply in scenarios where the person being removed from a home, dwelling or occupied vehicle is a child, grandchild, is under the lawful custody of, or is under the lawful guardianship of, the person against whom the deadly force is used. So again, you should carefully think before taking actions related to domestic family situations.

Also, as mentioned earlier, the two presumptions discussed above do not apply if you are engaged in an unlawful activity or are using the dwelling, residence, or occupied vehicle to further an unlawful activity. So, if you are using your home, dwelling, or vehicle for illegal activity, do not expect the Act to provide you with those presumptions.

Finally, the presumptions discussed above do not apply if the person against whom you use deadly force is a law enforcement officer who enters or attempts to enter the dwelling, residence, or occupied vehicle to perform his or her official duties. This is true as long as the officer identifies himself in accordance with applicable law or if you knew or should have known that the person was a law enforcement officer. Because police are trained to assume that homeowners, residents, and vehicle occupants have weapons, police generally enter these places very openly and with conspicuous notice. Therefore, it is unlikely that you will be confronted with a law enforcement officer in a castle doctrine situation. However, it can happen so make every reasonable effort to identify any person before you consider using deadly force against them.

The above exception is only applicable in the usual scenario where a law enforcement officer enters a home, dwelling or occupied vehicle to perform his or her official duties and with conspicuous notice. However, if a law enforcement officer enters a home, dwelling or occupied vehicle not under those circumstances, the person who uses deadly force against the officer is imputed with the presumptions provided for in the Act. Implicit in this exception is that the officer is not out of control, unlawfully out to kill or cause serious bodily harm to someone.

The Act has two additional provisions that we have not yet discussed. The first is Subsection (D) that reads:

(D) A person who unlawfully and by force enters or attempts to enter a person's dwelling, residence, or occupied vehicle is presumed to be doing so with the intent to commit an unlawful act involving force or a violent crime as defined in Section 16-1-60.

This section creates a presumption against the intruder. By the act of forcefully entering a dwelling, residence or occupied vehicle, the intruder is presumed to intend to commit one or more of a host of specified crimes. Technically, the Act imputes the intruder with the intent element necessary to convict that person for one or more of the following:

- Murder

- 1st & 2nd degree criminal sexual conduct (Rape)

- 1st & 2nd degree criminal sexual conduct with minors (Rape)

- 1st & 2nd degree assault with intent to commit criminal sexual conduct

- Assault and battery with intent to kill (Deadly threat or use of force)

- Kidnapping

- Voluntary manslaughter (Heat of Emotions Killing)

- Armed robbery

- Attempted armed robbery

- Carjacking

- Drug trafficking as defined in Sections 44-53-370(e), 44-53-375(C); or 44-53-375

- 1st & 2nd degree arson in the first degree

- 1st & 2nd degree burglary (breaking and entering a dwelling with the intent to commit a serious felony therein)

- Engaging a child for a sexual performance

- Homicide by child abuse, aiding and abetting homicide by child abuse, inflicting great bodily injury upon a child, or allowing great bodily injury to be inflicted upon a child

- Criminal domestic violence of a high and aggravated nature

- Abuse or neglect of a vulnerable adult resulting in death or great bodily injury

- Accessory before the fact to commit any of the above offenses

This is an added layer of legal protection for the victim of a crime that has to use deadly force in self-defense against an intruder.

Finally, the Act specifies that:

> (E) A person who by force enters or attempts to enter a dwelling, residence, or occupied vehicle in violation of an order of protection, restraining order, or condition of bond is presumed to be doing so with the intent to commit an unlawful act regardless of whether the person is a resident of the dwelling, residence, or occupied vehicle including, but not limited to, an owner, lessee, or titleholder.

Here is another example of the law going the extra mile to protect families against domestic violence. As we have repeated throughout this book, take special care to stay away from instances of domestic violence. This subsection imputes the intent to commit an unlawful act upon people that forcefully enter or attempt to enter dwellings, residences, and occupied vehicles in violation of a court order or bond condition. Generally this situation arises where one person in a relationship was able to go to a court and obtain an order preventing the other person from entering the dwelling or otherwise harassing the person protected by the order. A condition of bond might arise when someone is arrested for domestic violence and one of the conditions of getting out of jail on bond is that the person will not go around the alleged victim.

Under this subsection, the person breaking the conditions of an order or bond must not merely enter the dwelling, residence or occupied vehicle but must do so *forcefully* to be imputed with the presumption. It might be a criminal violation to break the order or condition but the imputation of intent to commit an unlawful act in the dwelling, residence or occupied vehicle only arises if the person enters or attempts to enter with force. In other words, if a sympathetic girlfriend lets her boyfriend with a restraining order into the house, and then the boyfriend becomes violent against the girlfriend, the boyfriend is not burdened with the presumption of intent to commit unlawful activity in the home. Therefore, if she is required to use deadly force against the boyfriend, she does not benefit from any presumption of intent to commit unlawful activity imputed upon the boyfriend.

In conclusion, the Act codifies the castle doctrine and provides beneficial presumptions to those lawfully in their residence, dwelling or occupied vehicle. It also allows you to stand your ground and use deadly force against the deadly threat in most circumstances. In the end, the Act provides a strengthened legal basis for your claim of self-defense if you are not engaging in unlawful activity and in a place where you are legally entitled to be.

Self-Defense against Non-Deadly Attacks

As to non-deadly force, you have no duty to retreat if you are not engaged in an unlawful activity and you are attacked in any place where you have the right to be. Therefore, if you are legally anywhere and acting lawfully, you can stand your ground and punch a guy back if he starts punching you. Be careful though because non-deadly force can escalate into deadly force. So, if someone attacks you with non-deadly force and you fight back but the encounter escalates to the point where you respond with deadly force, you cannot successfully raise a claim of self-defense if you are found to have escalated any portion of the encounter. It should be noted here that if there was mutual combat in the beginning, the chances of being without fault are pretty small.

Be aware that attacks occur in seconds. Generally, you will be required to discern the level of threat instantly and respond. Again, the legal standard that will be applied to you is that of a reasonable man or woman under the same or similar circumstances. This is not a subjective standard. In other words, a jury will not be asked to determine what you thought was reasonable but what a reasonable man would think. Do you understand the subtle difference? Your actions will be judged by what the jury determines is reasonable under the circumstances. In all situations, keen situational awareness will make you more prepared to react correctly.

The "Alter-Ego" Rule

When it comes to defending others, South Carolina follows the "Alter-Ego" rule. This means that, if you intervene on behalf of another, you will not be allowed the legal defense of self-defense unless self-defense would have been available to the person you assisted. Put another way, a person who intervenes for another is said to "stand in the shoes" of the person on whose behalf he is intervening.

What does this mean? If you encounter a person who is under a threat of imminent deadly harm, and you step in to help, you legally "stand in the shoes" of that person. Therefore, if all four of the elements of legal self-defense are present for that person, you are also protected by that legal defense.

The Danger of Defending Others under the Alter-Ego Rule

There is a very dangerous aspect of the alter-ego rule. The person whom you attempt to assist must have the right to use self-defense under the situation. So, go back to the first element that must be present for legal defense: you must be without fault in bringing on the difficulty. When you "step into the shoes" of the person you are defending, you take the risk that the person you are defending has some fault in the episode.

Here is a factual scenario: say that you come around a corner and see a guy pointing a gun at a woman and he is saying that he will shoot her. You shoot the guy, and seriously injure him. The attack ends and the woman runs away. You then notice that she has a gun in the hand of the arm that was blocked from your view by her torso. Witnesses indicate that she was robbing the guy at gunpoint and that he responded by drawing his gun on her. Under these facts, you legally stepped into the woman's shoes but she did not have the legal defense of self-defense because the woman was not without fault in causing the man to draw his gun.

Preventing the Commission of a Violent Crime

You have no duty to retreat and you can use deadly force as long as you reasonably believe that your use of deadly force is necessary to prevent death, great bodily harm or to prevent the commission of a violent crime as defined by Section 16-1-60 of the South Carolina Code of Laws.

Protecting Yourself or Others versus Protecting Property

You can only use deadly force to prevent the use of deadly force upon you or someone else. You must have a reasonable fear that you or someone else is about to get killed or be seriously injured. You cannot use deadly force to stop non-deadly force. You cannot use deadly force to protect property. To protect property, you can only use non-deadly force. Therefore, if you reasonably believe that someone is threatening your property but not your person or someone else's person, you can only protect your property with non-deadly force.

This might sound like a contradiction to the Protection of Persons and Property Act because that Act allows you to use deadly force to prevent certain attacks and invasions upon a dwelling. The confusion arises by the fact that real estate is often called "property" and dwellings are often referred to as "my property." When we say that you cannot use deadly force to protect property, we are referring to personal property and unoccupied real estate. When the Act refers to property, it refers to occupied homes, dwellings and private conveyances (cars, boats, motorcycles, private airplanes, etc.).

As an example of personal property or unoccupied real estate, look back to our earlier discussion of trap or spring guns. Spring guns are devices rigged-up to go off if someone opens a door or lifts a cover. Historically, some people have installed trap guns to protect their property when the occupants are away. These devices are illegal because they are primarily designed to use deadly force to protect unoccupied property.

We live in a flawed world and the courts cannot monitor and fully understand every situation that happens. For this reason, the law creates certain principles. One principle is that life is always more important than things. Therefore, a court will never give you a pass for killing or causing serious bodily injury where only possessions are in danger.

Arson is a unique crime because it is a crime against property but there is a high likelihood of someone being burned in the flames. For instance, homes and businesses often have people in them around the clock. Therefore, even if the arsonist believes that someone is not in the building, there remains a very good chance that someone actually is in the building. Further, people who try to put the fire out can be seriously hurt or killed in the attempt. For these reasons, arson is generally not considered simply a property crime but also a crime of violence.

Can an altercation over possessions escalate from non-deadly force to deadly force? Yes it can. You can initially resist a property theft with non-deadly force. Thereafter, the thief's threat against you can become deadly. Maybe he or she later pulls a gun or knife or tries to run you over with a car. Maybe a thief places someone near you in a deadly choke hold. The iterations are endless. A non-deadly threat can escalate into a deadly threat.

Make sure that you understand this principle that the law puts life above things. You can never use deadly force to protect personal property or unoccupied real estate. Only non-deadly force can be used to protect these things. However, the act of protecting your property with non-deadly force can escalate into a deadly situation. If you are faced with a situation where the property threat has escalated into a deadly threat to you or others, you can use deadly force for legitimate self-defense. Again though, keep in mind that you must have the four elements of legal self-defense working in your favor anytime you use deadly force against another.

Criminal and Civil Liability

This book contains a more thorough presentation and analysis of common ways that a gun can get you into criminal and civil trouble in the Common Gun Crimes and Lawsuits chapter. However, for the purpose of this chapter, some criminal and civil liability concepts are briefly presented here.

Complete Defense to Criminal and Civil Action

If you shoot someone in legitimate self-defense, you have the affirmative defense of self-defense in any subsequent criminal charge. Further, you are protected from civil liability. In fact, the law provides that if you lawfully defend yourself, any person who sues you will end up having to pay your attorney's fees, court costs, all expenses associated

189

with the lawsuit, plus any lost income as a result of the lawsuit. Unfortunately, if that person has little collectible money or property, you will probably never get a penny out of them.

Excusable Homicide

There are a few situations where you may kill someone (not in self-defense) but you are still not guilty of murder or manslaughter. These cases are called excusable homicide. Let's say you are out downtown doing some shopping and someone pulls a gun on you and starts shooting. You fire back. You fire three shots. The first two hit and kill the assailant. The third goes slightly off target and kills a guy who is typing on his laptop in an overpriced coffee shop. Since you were justified in shooting at the first guy and since you did not intend to hit the second guy, the likely result is a finding of excusable homicide. Self-defense would apply to the first killing and excusable homicide would apply to the second killing. More common scenarios are accidental killings from gun cleaning and hunting accidents. The bottom line is that accidental shootings are generally excusable homicide.

However, some accidental shootings will not be excused by the criminal courts. There is no excuse for acting grossly negligent. For example, someone shoots a gun in the air for a New Year's celebration. The bullet then comes down on the other side of town and kills someone. That type of behavior is so reckless and wanton that it rises to gross negligence and brings both criminal and civil liability. There are many other ways to be grossly negligent with a gun.

Criminal Manslaughter

Manslaughter is the killing of another but with some mitigating factor or factors. Say for instance that you think that you have a reason to shoot another person but you are wrong. As an example, a guy across the street has a tire iron in his hand and yells threats to kill you without making any attempt to cross the street towards you. He also says things that highly inflame you. As a response to his threats, you shoot and kill him. In this case, his threat of deadly force is not imminent enough.

However, the law has a means for cutting you somewhat of a break. That break is a manslaughter charge, as opposed to a murder charge. Manslaughter is killing another with some mitigating factor such as high emotions or heat of passion. Maybe a jury finds that his words and actions caused you to be highly enraged and it is reasonable that your emotions were inflamed. That determination might move you out of murder liability and into the lesser penalized manslaughter liability. In any case, whether you are tried for murder, manslaughter or nothing is a decision for the prosecutor and possibly the judge to make. Whether you are guilty or not is for the jury to decide.

Civil Negligence

A broad theory for recovery of damages in a civil lawsuit is negligence. Negligence is when a person's actions fall below the standard of care that should have been used in a particular situation. If you use a weapon for legitimate self-defense under the law, the Protection of Persons and Property Act aids you in defense of a civil claim like negligence. If you have acted in legitimate self-defense under the Act, the civil lawsuit should be dismissed by the judge and you should be awarded the cost of your attorney's fees for defending yourself against the lawsuit.

Display of Weapons

You might be wondering when it is legal to pull a gun out and threaten someone. It is very simple, if it is not legal to shoot the person, it is also not legal to pull your gun and threaten to shoot the person. While threatening will not get you a murder charge, it will get you an aggravated assault charge. Aggravated assault is a felony and getting convicted will mean you can't own a gun. Remember, if the situation does not legally warrant shooting a person, it is a crime to threaten to shoot the person. Therefore, you should always be of the mindset that you will not pull out your weapon unless you, or someone else you are defending, are faced with the threat of death or serious bodily injury.

What if I Shoot Someone in Self-Defense?

If you have been forced to shoot someone in self-defense, you have to consider competing concerns. First, there is the concern for the safety of you and others. Second, is the concern for the person who has been shot. Third, you have to balance the need to give the police some very limited information against your right to remain silent.

For your own safety, or the safety of those you have defended, you should get to a safe place away from the person that you have shot. Once you determine that you are safe and the person is no longer a threat, make sure that someone calls the police. If anybody decides to give aid to anybody who has been shot, the aid or assistance given must meet the level of care that any ordinary and reasonable person would be expected to give under the same or similar circumstances. In light of South Carolina's Good Samaritan Law found in Section 15-1-310 of the South Carolina Code of Laws, this means that the care cannot be reckless or wanton.

Why You Must Never Talk with the Police or Anyone Else

(Author's note: the following section is written solely by the two attorney authors.)

When the police come, tell them your name and give them your driver's license or other ID and your CWP if you have one. After that, demand to speak with a lawyer and do not say anything else. Period. Demand to speak with a lawyer and **DO NOT SAY ANYTHING ELSE.**

When we say do not *say* anything, that also means do not write any letters or reports or sign anything. Further, do not make any apologies, agree to any "interviews," or talk with any reporters or bystanders. This includes not giving any statement to your family or friends.

We cannot stress strongly enough the importance of forcing yourself to not say anything and simply demanding an attorney. While there are several good reasons, following are two of the strongest: first, our system of criminal justice is an imperfect system that has plenty of room for error and wrong results beyond your control. Law-abiding, innocent people can be found guilty as a result of the peculiarities and mechanics of the system. Forcing yourself not to say anything and demanding an attorney minimizes the chance of a wrong outcome. Second, people have a compelling urge to talk after a traumatic event occurs – especially if the person is involved in the event. Forcing yourself not to say anything and demanding an attorney overcomes this urge and minimizes the chance of a wrong outcome.

United States Supreme Court Justice Robert Jackson said in Watts v. Indiana, "under [our system] of criminal procedure, any lawyer worth his salt will tell the suspect in no uncertain terms to make no statement to the police under any circumstances." This is an expert in American Constitutional Law writing an opinion for a real case before the Supreme Court. He had an impressive history of litigating prominent national cases before being appointed to the Supreme Court. Even if indirectly, you must take his comment as a stark warning of the severe prejudice that will come from not remaining silent. Listen to his words again, "in no uncertain terms, make no statement to the police under any circumstances."

Here is a thought experiment to try. Find a quiet place, close your eyes and go through the next scenario several times in your head. Pretend that you are in a convenience store at night when three masked people suddenly come in to rob the place. One starts to point a gun at you and you fear for your life so you shoot and hit the robber. The other two robbers flee. You have just shot someone in lawful self-defense. The police arrive and approach you. You are scared and in shock but happy to see the police. You are a law abiding person and you like the police and are eager to cooperate with the authorities.

How do you feel right now? Do you have an urge to tell the police something? Is there an urge to explain yourself? Do you want the police to think that you are cooperating? Do you want the police to like you? Do you feel uncomfortable just standing there not answering questions from the police? Do you think that if you don't say something to the police they will think that you are trying to hide something? Would you have an urge to respond if you hear the clerk tell wrong facts to the police? Do you feel like the police would not arrest you if you tell them what happened? Do you think it will all just go away and that an attorney will only make a bigger deal out of the situation? Do you worry that an attorney will be too expensive? All of those thoughts are normal but they bitterly betray your best interest.

The vast majority of police and prosecutors are very dedicated professionals who do an excellent job of protecting us everyday. They generally want to help law abiding citizens. But you must understand their role in our criminal justice system. Our society has placed the responsibility of prosecuting suspected crimes upon the prosecutor and the responsibility of gathering as much evidence as possible on the police. They would be derelict in their jobs if they did not gather as much evidence as possible and use the criminal justice system to its fullest legal effect against the accused. Being a creature of the state, they have tremendous resources and training and receive a high degree of respect and credulity from juries. Also, a trial might not occur until a year or more after the shooting. The police officer's interpretation of what you said can change over time or prosecuting attorneys can develop alternate arguments based upon the way you worded the story. Last, but certainly not least, as we will explain more fully below, the rules of evidence **can only work <u>against</u> you** and not for you if you open your mouth and speak with someone. The point is, the rules are against you right from the start and you are up against a behemoth. The most vulnerable time is the time between the shooting and the time that your attorney arrives by your side. In the next sections we will discuss some of the things that can happen if you decide to talk with the police (or anybody else).

To help you see how the rules will work against you and not for you, consider the South Carolina rules of evidence. South Carolina follows the general rule that hearsay is not admissible as evidence in a trial. What is hearsay? Hearsay is *a statement, other than one made by the declarant while testifying at trial or hearing, offered in evidence to prove the truth of the matter asserted.* How does this rule apply to a statement that you make to the police? Let's say that you were involved in a self-defense shooting and you speak with the police and that the only thing that you tell them was that, "I was in fear for my life." Now say that you are at trial for shooting the attacker and that you have raised the defense of self-defense. An element of self-defense is that you were in reasonable fear of imminent death or serious bodily injury. The policeman that you spoke with is called to the witness stand. If your attorney asks the officer to repeat what you said, that officer cannot say that you said, "I was in fear for my life," because that testimony is inadmissible as hearsay. Why? Your statement was not made at trial and it is being offered as evidence to prove the matter asserted (that you were in fear for your life). So, your statement to the police that you were in fear for your life will not help you at trial. Notice how it is the *rule* working against you and not the police officer. The officer might believe that you are innocent and might hope that the jury acquits you. But, no matter how decent and nice the police office is, or how much the officer is "on your side," it is the rule working against you and not the officer.

While that news is bad enough, the real bad news is that there are important exceptions to the general hearsay rule. The one you need to know about here is that any disserving statements or admissions that you make **are admissible** as evidence. So, even if you are completely innocent, you might say things to the police that can later be presented to a jury as a disserving statement or an admission of guilt. You might say the most trivial things or convincingly explain your innocence with thorough detail, but the way you say something could be interpreted by a jury as an admission. You should never run that risk. Never! Keep quiet and let the facts speak for themselves.

The foregoing should be enough to convince you not to talk with the police under any circumstance. Again, this is not an indictment against the police but rather a simple fact of the mechanics of the rules of evidence and the justice system. The *Miranda* warning tells you that anything that you say, can and will be used against you in court. But, the warning fails to inform you that nothing that you say can or will be used to help you in court. In other words, the rules are rigged so that any statement that you make can only hurt you but never help you.

But, if the foregoing reason was not enough, let's go though some more reasons. Let's imagine again that you were forced to shoot somebody who presented you with an imminent threat of death or serious bodily harm. You then find safety and call the police. The person that presented you with the threat survives the shooting. When the police come, you say nothing until an attorney is by your side. If it ever comes to a trial, there should be facts to back you up. Maybe there were also witnesses there that will back you up. If only the attacker and you were on the scene, it is simply your version of the episode against the other guy's and you have made no statements that can be used against you.

Now let's change the facts and say that you said some things to the police. What if the officer misinterprets a word because of your accent or the manner in which you said something? What if the officer had an impression of you that is not correct? What if the officer mistakenly writes a statement down differently from what you said? What if an officer recalls your statement differently because a year has passed by before a trial begins? Once you say something to the police, it becomes your word against the other guy AND the police at trial. By talking with the police (or anybody else) without having an attorney by your side first, you have doubled the risk of a wrong outcome through witness error. If you talk with more people, including family and friends, before waiting until you have a lawyer by your side, you triple, or quadruple the risk. What do we mean by witness error? Witness error is communication malfunctions and people make mistakes in communication all of the time. People misinterpret information, forget things, see things through their own world view, import prejudices, can develop ulterior motives, and can simply lie at times.

Maybe you have played the communication game that starts with a classroom full of people sitting quietly. The teacher whispers a phrase into one student's ear at one side of the room. That student leans over and whispers the phrase to the student next to him or her. The phrase is passed from desk to desk, up and down each row, until the phrase reaches the last student at the far end of the room. The teacher then tells the last student to close his or her eyes while the teacher writes the phrase on the board. The last student is then told to shout out the phrase. Invariably, a burst of laughter erupts because the shouted phrase is nothing close to the original phrase. The message became corrupted and distorted through human communication. While this communication gets a lot of laughs in school, witness error through miscommunication is not funny when somebody is facing serious criminal charges.

Police are only allowed to convey the statements that they were given. If you say nothing to the police, you give the officer and jury no room to misinterpret your words. The officer will likely give a brief testimony of the facts on the scene and will offer up no statement that can be subjected to damaging examination by lawyers. Alternatively, if you talked to the officer, your words or statements are open to mistakes, misinterpretations, jury prejudices and damaging examination by attorneys. Moreover, the general public tends to hold the police in very high regard so juries tend to believe the testimony of a crisply dressed police officer more than others.

You will greatly simplify your defense if you are only required to contend with the guy that you were forced to shoot. In a practical sense, if it is your word against the other guy's, and your attorney is able to discredit the other guy, the prosecutor's case is all but lost. Similarly, if the other guy simply doesn't show up to court or refuses to testify, the prosecutor has no witnesses and the case has a good chance of getting dropped. So, why would you disadvantage yourself by talking with anyone?

Still another reason is that talking to the police will not keep you from getting arrested. For shootings, police make arrests based upon the evidence and the circumstances at the scene. The decision is almost never based upon what you say or do not say. If the police arrive and see one guy shot and you there possessing the gun that shot him, they are very likely going to make an arrest and your words will not get you out of the arrest. If you are arrested, you will spend some time in a holding cell and be required to post a bond. Nobody likes the disgusting smell, obnoxious drunks and baloney sandwiches in holding cells but that awful experience comes and goes relatively quickly and you can handle that. Arrests can even be expunged from your record. But, if you say anything to the police or anyone else, you can never get those words back and they will cause you much more grief than an arrest.

Yet another thing that can go wrong is that you might make inadvertent inaccuracies in your statement that are later used to attack your truthfulness and credibility. For instance, you tell the police that three guys barged into the convenience store, one started to point his gun at you and you feared for your life. As you try to describe the incident in more detail, you say that all three of the guys had guns. It turns out that only two of the guys had guns and the other had a thin aluminum can that he grabbed off the shelf. Even though it is an insignificant fact, a prosecutor can use your incorrect observation to attack your judgment and credibility.

Know also that the police are allowed to lie to you or deceive you to get you to make a confession. For example, the police can have a cassette recorder at your conversation and then stop the recorder to have some discussion "off the record." What they do not tell you is that you are being videotaped or that another recorder is running. Alternatively, you might have sympathy for the person that was injured or that person's family. Maybe you think that reaching out by saying you're sorry will make you feel better or somehow help the grieving family. The police might suggest that writing a sympathy letter or apology will make you feel better. You can be sure that your sympathy letter or apology will be turned into a confession. Just like you train to be better at your job, police go through extensive training to extract the maximum comments from you. You must protect yourself against saying anything.

As an additional indication of the built-in disadvantage of talking to the police, think of the dynamics of a post-shooting questioning. Again, you are upset, frightened, and probably surrounded by a growing crowd of onlookers. You want to get out of there and go home right away. Alternatively, the police are comfortably at work. They have all the time in the world. In-fact, as time goes on they start getting paid overtime. Since they are already uniformed and working, they might be happy to get a few more hours at time and a-half. Meanwhile, you are wishing you were home in your favorite chair. All of the pressure is on you to say something that you think will get you out of there. You must resist the urge to give your side of the story or to seem cooperative in the hope that the police will release you from the scene.

This might be a good place to talk about the length of time from a shooting until you have an attorney by your side. That period of time is dependent upon what type of relationship you have with an attorney. An organized crime kingpin probably has his criminal attorney's number listed as a favorite in his cell phone. When he calls his attorney, the attorney is at the scene within a matter of minutes. However, most people do not have a close relationship with a criminal attorney. So, realistically, the first thing that you will have to do is decide upon a lawyer to call. That decision might take some time because of asking references or thumbing though advertisements. After you decide upon an attorney, more variables come into play. Is the attorney available when you call? Does that attorney have a conflict of interest? How far away from the scene is the attorney's office? Is it rush hour? Does the attorney make jail calls? All of these variables have an effect upon when the attorney can first be by your side. So, the answer is that it can range from minutes to days. No matter if it is minutes or days, do not speak with the police without a lawyer by your side.

So, remain silent because silence might prevent you from saying something that will get you in trouble (even though you have done nothing wrong). Attorneys can work a lot more effectively with your silence than with comments that you have made. There is an old saying among lawyers that it is hard to hook the fish that never opens his mouth.

The best practice is to not give statements to ANYONE until your attorney arrives. Even if you do not give statements to the police, you can still give problematic statements to others on the scene. Anything that you say to anyone can and will be used against you in court. If your family or friends are with you, make an agreement that it is in everyone's best interest not to say anything until your attorney arrives. Even your family and friends can misinterpret things that you say. Imagine how terrible a friend or family member will feel if they have to get up on the stand and repeat something really stupid that you said? Do not put that burden on them. Keep quiet and do not give any statements until you have your attorney at the scene. You will have plenty of time to speak with your family and friends once your attorney arrives and everything settles down.

Trust in the facts on the scene and the circumstances that led to your use of deadly force in self-defense. There will likely be physical evidence and witnesses to back you up so why not just sit quietly until you get a lawyer beside you? The fact that you sat quietly until you had the assistance of legal counsel can never be used against you in court. Resist the natural temptation to explain yourself because remaining silent will only help you and never hurt you. Best advice, do not be the guy who painfully joked in jail, "I had the right to remain silent, just not the intelligence to do so."

One last note, if you safely have the opportunity to do so, call 911 as the life-threatening situation is developing. That way, a dispatcher might hear and record the situation as it unfolds. Also, calling 911 will show that you tried to get help from the police before the situation escalated to deadly force. Make it clear that you are in fear for your life. Keep 911 as a speed dial in your cell phone and use it if you can.

Remember that every defendant is entitled to an attorney. If you cannot afford a private attorney, a public defender attorney will be provided for you. So, whether you hire a private attorney or have a public defender appointed for you, there is no excuse not to have an attorney by your side.

Recapping this section, what do you do if you shot someone in legitimate self defense?

1. Find safety right away.
2. Put your gun back into your holster or pocket.

3. Give the police your name, address, and driver's license or other ID and your CWP if you have one.

4. DO NOT TALK TO THE POLICE OR ANYONE and say you want a lawyer.

Bottom line: you must follow Justice Jackson's admonition: **"in no uncertain terms, make no statement to the police under any circumstances."**

Homeowner's, Auto, and Umbrella Insurance Policies

Homeowner's insurance and business liability insurance policies generally have a personal liability provision. Many people also have "umbrella" liability policies that supplement and increase liability coverage. In general, these policies provide liability indemnification for occurrences at the home or business, in or about a vehicle or even elsewhere in public. Be aware that these policies insure against the *negligent* acts of the insured and not the intentional acts of the insured. The use of a weapon in self-defense is considered intentional and will not be covered by these insurance policies. So, if you are sued, you will not be provided an attorney by your insurance company and you will not be covered for any judgment against you. As mentioned earlier, the South Carolina Code of Laws give you complete relief from civil liability if you use deadly force in lawful self-defense. As far as your insurance carrier is concerned though, you will have to hire your own attorney.

Simple Rules for Making Sense of Self-Defense

You might feel like the law of self-defense is more complicated than you would like. It is. But it probably has to be to balance the individual's need to protect him or herself against the public's need for a civilized community. Again, the best practice is to start organizing your thoughts now into a few simple rules for yourself. If you live by these simple rules, it is very difficult for you to face criminal or civil liability:

- Do not start or escalate trouble with other people. If you do make a mistake and start trouble, eat your pride and get away before it escalates any further and deadly force comes into use. Remember that you must be without fault throughout the entire episode to successfully raise the affirmative defense of self-defense if you use deadly force;

- Never draw your gun unless you legitimately feel like you or someone else is in immediate danger of death or serious bodily injury;

- If you step in to use your gun in defense of another, you better be sure that the person you are defending is without fault throughout the entire episode.

- If you shoot someone, demand an attorney right away and do not speak with anyone until he or she is at your side.

Conclusion

You have a right to defend yourself but you must understand when and how you can do so. Your attitude should always be that your weapon is for defense and that you will pull it out from concealment and use it only when the circumstances legitimately necessitate it. Your actions will not be judged by whether you think they are reasonable but rather by what a jury thinks a reasonable person would do under the same or similar circumstances. Knowledge of the law of self-defense should give you confidence to carry your weapon legally and intelligently. This knowledge should also make you not afraid of the law if you need to use your weapon against a legitimate immediate threat of death or serious bodily injury.

203

Summary Points

- An alert mind and keen situational awareness are your first line of self-defense.

- The law makes a distinction between deadly force and non-deadly force and this distinction is very important.

- You may use *non*-deadly force to protect your possessions and to protect yourself and others from the imminent use of non-deadly force by another.

- You may use deadly force to protect yourself and others from the imminent use of deadly force by another.

- Any use of force must be reasonable under the circumstances.

- You will be judged by the "reasonable man" standard.

- If you step in to help defend someone, you will face liability if that person started or escalated the encounter.

- There are presumptions that are imposed by law under certain circumstances.

- Law-abiding citizens do not have a duty to retreat under most circumstances.

- If your use of force is reasonable and allowed, you are protected from criminal and civil prosecution.

- If you shoot someone, demand to have your attorney and do not speak with the police or anyone until your attorney is at your side.

Chapter 8
Miscellaneous Gun Related Laws

The Shooting Range Protection Act of 2000

Section 31-18-20 of the South Carolina Code of Laws defines a shooting range as an area of a property which is designed, utilized, and operated for the firing of firearms. Also, in order for an area to be a shooting range; the firing of firearms must be the usual, regular, and primary activity occurring in the area. Finally, the area must be remote enough so that a projectile could not reasonably be expected to escape the boundaries of the range. Alternatively, the range must have a sufficient barrier that would have the same effect. If the range meets these criteria, it is a shooting range for purposes of the Act. The main thrust of the Act is to limit noise nuisance lawsuits against shooting ranges by neighboring landowners.

There are several situations which must be considered when analyzing this Act. First, consider the situation where the complaining party buys property near the range after the range is already operating. In those instances, the complainer is not allowed to bring a noise nuisance suit against the shooting range, the owners of the shooting range, the operators of the range, or the users of the range unless there is a substantial change in the use of the property. Even if there is such a substantial change in the use of the property, a noise nuisance lawsuit must be brought within three years from the beginning of the substantial change.

Next is when a neighbor complains that a range is established after the complainer already owned the nearby property. In this situation, any noise nuisance action must be brought within five years after the establishment of the range or within three years after a substantial change in the use of the range. If a range stops all shooting activity for a period of at least three years, any resumption of shooting activities is considered establishment of a new range for purposes of the Act. The three year period is tolled if all shooting activity ceases due to legal action against the range, its owners, its operators, or its users.

In addition to the limits that the Act places on lawsuits, the legislation also limits control over shooting ranges by local governments. First, it forbids local and state government agencies from using a noise control ordinance, regulation, or rule to require a shooting range to limit or eliminate shooting activities if the range has been operating on a regular basis since January 1, 2000. It also forbids local and state government agencies from applying noise control ordinances, regulations, and rules to a shooting range if that shooting range was in compliance with all noise control ordinances, regulations, and rules in effect when it was established. This protection endures so long as there has not been a substantial change in the use of the range. Finally, a local or state government agency may not apply any noise control ordinance, regulation, or rule to a shooting range if the range was in existence prior to the enactment of the regulation. Again, this is true as long as there has been no substantial change in the use of the range.

The act does not limit the ability of a local government to regulate the location and construction of a new shooting range. Further, the Act requires county governments to prominently display a warning sign on all primary highways approaching a range. At a one mile radius from each shooting range, a sign must be erected that reads,

"SHOOTING RANGE~NOISE AREA". The warning sign must also conform to the Manual of Uniform Traffic Control Devices and the policies of the Department of Transportation.

Civil Lawsuit Protection for Gun and Ammunition Manufacturers

Section 15-73-40 of the South Carolina Code of Laws gives gun and ammunition manufacturers greater protection from civil lawsuits. This statute was enacted as a response to increased products liability lawsuits against gun and ammunition manufacturers. Plaintiffs began bringing defective product lawsuits against manufacturers not founded on a basis of individual guns being mechanically defective but rather on other grounds like the inherently dangerous nature of guns. This statute provides that any defective product case must be based upon a firearm being either defectively designed or constructed. Further, for a plaintiff to sustain a product liability lawsuit, the defective design or construction must be the proximate cause of the injury or death.

Local Governments cannot Confiscate Guns during an Emergency

Section 23-31-520 has been amended to prevent counties, cities and other political subdivisions like special districts from confiscating guns during an emergency. After the Hurricane Katrina damage in Louisiana, the City of New Orleans authorized law enforcement officers to go door-to-door confiscating firearms from private citizens. Guns were confiscated from individuals at their homes with no allegation of any wrongdoing. The goal was simply to disarm private citizens as a result of the state of emergency. This action shocked the conscience of many who assumed that governments would not confiscate guns from law abiding citizens expecting the protection of a firearm during an emergency.

Twenty-three states including South Carolina responded by either enacting new laws or amending existing laws to prevent local governments from confiscating firearms. South Carolina did not limit the confiscation prohibition to just emergencies. Instead, the local government preemption law discussed in Chapter 1 was amended to include the following language urged by GrassRoots GunRights, "[t]his article denies any county, municipality, or political subdivision the power to confiscate a firearm or ammunition unless incident to an arrest or a courtesy summons to appear." (A courtesy summons to appear is a notice to appear before the court for formal criminal charges without a law enforcement officer actually handcuffing and hauling the suspect to jail.)

The effect of this law is to prevent local governments from confiscating guns from a private party unless in coincidence with some type of criminal charges. No matter if an emergency is occurring or not, a local government in South Carolina cannot go around confiscating guns unless the persons who they are confiscating from violated some criminal laws and are being arrested for the violation.

Remember earlier that we said that a local government cannot make a gun law more restrictive or at odds with state law. Therefore, a local government cannot get around this confiscation provision by making up a gun law more restrictive than state law and then confiscating a gun during an arrest for that local government regulation. So, Legislative Consultant Robert D. Butler did a great job of recommending language for this law that prevents local governments from attempting to confiscate guns from law abiding citizens during an emergency.

Assault Weapons Ban

In 1994 Congress passed what is commonly called the assault weapons ban. As part of a larger crime bill, the legislation defined "assault rifle" and made the manufacture, importation, and possession of assault rifles (manufactured or imported after enactment) illegal. It is important to note that the weapons banned were not fully automatic machine guns like the Army and Marines take into battle. Instead, the highly political bill attempted to demonize semi-automatic guns that only looked like military assault rifles with the label "assault rifles." The bill also outlawed the sale of normal capacity magazines by allowing only reduced capacity magazines capable of holding no more than ten cartridges. The "assault weapons" ban ended on September 13, 2004 and is no longer the law of the land.

The "assault rifles" banned were generally semiautomatic weapons that are readily available today in gun shops. Expiration of the law does not mean that you can buy or possess machine guns and other military weapons. It does, however, allow you to purchase many military style rifles in semi-automatic-only configurations with the normal magazines designed for the rifles (i.e. 25-30 round capacity).

Making Modifications to Semi-Automatic Assault Rifles

Modifying assault type weapons can be a tricky legal endeavor. You are well advised to not make modifications to an assault type

weapon without thoroughly studying the applicable law. Even after considerable study, many attorneys are left scratching their heads. But you can be sure that federal prosecutors will be able to prosecute violations when they need to. Do not modify, or have someone else modify, assault weapons unless you are completely sure that your modifications are legal.

A thorough analysis of modifications is beyond the scope of this book. If you want to do further study, a good place to start is on the internet. There are several books written solely for the purpose of explaining the law of modifying semi-automatic rifles. You can also go to the primary sources of the federal statutes and implementing regulations. Following are the cites: 18 USC 922(r), 18 USC 925(d)(3), Section 5845(a) of the Internal Revenue Code, 27 CFR 478.39 and 479, and 58 Federal Register 40587 (July 29, 1993). Reading these sections is almost as fun as reading the tax code.

The Law Enforcement Officers Safety Act

The U.S. Congress passed the Law Enforcement Officers Safety Act in 2004. Under the Act, a current or retired law enforcement officer can carry a concealed firearm in any U.S. state or territory. The authorization comes with some conditions.

Federal statute 18 USC 926B sets forth the parameters for currently employed officers. First, the officer must be a currently qualified law enforcement officer employed by a state, county or municipality. When carrying a concealed weapon, the officer must carry his or her government issued photographic law enforcement identification. This allows carry anywhere in the United States and territories. The Act does not apply to machine guns, silencers, and destructive devices.

A qualified law enforcement officer is an employee of a governmental law enforcement agency who:

- is authorized by law to engage in or supervise the prevention, detection, investigation, or prosecution of, or the incarceration of any person for, any violation of law, and has statutory powers of arrest;

- is authorized by the agency to carry a firearm;

- is not the subject of any disciplinary action by the agency;

- meets the standards, if any, established by the agency which require the employee to regularly qualify in the use of a firearm;

- is not under the influence of alcohol or another intoxicating or hallucinatory drug or substance; and,

- is not prohibited by federal law from receiving a firearm.

Make sure that you are qualified under these rules if you want to carry.

The Act does not usurp any state law that restricts possession of concealed weapons on private property or government property. Therefore, out of state officers in South Carolina who encounter businesses with properly installed "no concealed carry" signs should not carry in those stores. Likewise, out of state officers should abide by all other South Carolina laws regarding concealed carry on private property or government property. If the officer is on duty, the officer falls under the rules for officers on duty. The officer must follow all federal firearms restrictions at all times. Remember that this rule allows for concealed carry by qualified officers. Officers carrying under this rule should not open carry as they would while on duty.

Retired officers are covered under 18 USC 926(C). Basically, the restrictions are the same for current officers. However, the retired officers must meet the following conditions:

- The officer must be retired in good standing from service with a public agency as a law enforcement officer;

- retirement from the public agency must not have been for reasons of mental instability;

- before retirement, the officer must have been authorized by law to engage in or supervise the prevention, detection, investigation, or prosecution of, or the incarceration of any person for, any violation of law, and had statutory powers of arrest;

- before retirement, the officer was regularly employed as a law enforcement officer for an aggregate of 15 years or more; or retired from service after completing any applicable probationary period of such service, due to a service-connected disability, as determined by such agency;

- the officer has a non-forfeitable right to benefits under the retirement plan of the agency;

- during the most recent 12-month period, the officer has met, at the expense of the individual, his or her state's standards for training and qualification for active law enforcement officers to carry firearms;

- is not under the influence of alcohol or another intoxicating or hallucinatory drug or substance; and,

- is not prohibited by Federal law from receiving a firearm.

Further, the retired officer must have the following identification:

- a photographic identification issued by the agency from which the officer retired from service that indicates that the individual has, not less than one year before the date the officer is carrying the concealed firearm, been tested or otherwise found by the agency to meet the standards established by the agency for training and qualification for active law enforcement officers to carry a firearm of the same type as the concealed firearm; **or**

- a photographic identification issued by the agency from which the officer retired from service as a law enforcement officer; **and,**

- a certification issued by the State in which the officer resides that indicates that the retired officer has, not less recently than one year before the date the officer is carrying the concealed firearm, been tested or otherwise found by the state to meet the standards established by the state for training and qualification for active law enforcement officers to carry a firearm of the same type as the concealed firearm.

So, retired officers need both a certificate of firearms qualifying within a year and a government issued photo identification showing that you are a retired law enforcement officer meeting all the other requirements of this statute.

Section 23-31-600 of the South Carolina Code of Laws requires all South Carolina law enforcement agencies to issue qualified retired officers the applicable identification card and documentation of training. This section implements the federal law and creates a statutory mandate for South Carolina agencies. It also provides agencies with authorization to charge a reasonable fee for the cost of processing.

Under this Act, current and retired officers need to be careful about carrying a concealed weapon outside of their own state. One thing to consider is that the officer must know the places where carry is prohibited under the laws of the other state. Another consideration is that many states provide which private individuals and businesses can prohibit concealed carry on private property. Remember too the federal rules about not carrying in the sterile area of airports and on commercial aircraft and public transportation.

Proposed National Right to Carry Law

Since 1995, Congressman Cliff Stearns, a Republican from Florida, has been introducing some form of a national right to carry bill in the U.S. House of Representatives. Stearns' current version is H.R. 197. The bill would allow a person with a valid concealed firearm carrying permit, issued by any one state, to carry a concealed firearm in all of the other states, under the following rules:

- in states that issue concealed firearm permits, that state's laws governing where concealed firearms may be carried would apply within its borders;

- in states that do not issue carry permits, a simplified federal standard would permit carrying in most places with the exception of police stations, courthouses, public polling places, meetings of state, county, or municipal governing bodies, schools, passenger areas of airports, and certain other locations.

The law would apply to Washington, D.C., Puerto Rico and U.S. territories abroad but would not create a federal licensing system. Instead, it would require a state to recognize all other states' carry permits, just as they currently recognize drivers' licenses.

Security Officers and Private Security Companies

Private security companies, security officers and private investigators are regulated and licensed under South Carolina law. The statutory provisions regarding these entities begin at Section 40-18-20. SLED executes the provisions of Section 40-18-20 through regulations starting in Article 9, 73-400, South Carolina Code of Regulations. SLED issues two different licenses: the Security Weapons Permit and the Security *Concealed* Weapons Permit. Please note that these permits are wholly separate from the concealed weapons permit issued under 23-31-205, South Carolina Code of Laws and discussed in Chapter 4 of this book. Do not confuse the two.

Security Weapons Permit

Under this statute (40-18-20, et seq.), SLED may grant a Security Weapons Permit to carry a particular type of firearm to a person who is at least twenty-one years of age, is eligible to possess firearms, and is licensed or registered as a security officer. Application for the permit must be made on SLED forms available at: http://www.sled.sc.gov/PILicense.aspx?MenuID=PI. The fee for private security officer initial registration is $110.00.

Applicants must submit with the application one complete set of the applicant's fingerprints on SLED fingerprint cards. Just like for the Concealed Weapons Permit application, make sure that you use SLED fingerprint cards for the application. The permit is for one year and renewal applications are available on the SLED website or by calling SLED.

Applicants must also submit proof of training. The standard basic training course consists of four or more hours of training by a certified private security company training officer and must consist of the latest material provided to the trainer by the South Carolina Technical College Private Security Training School. The basic training must be completed, a written examination administered and scored, accurate results of the testing documented in the employer's files, and application for registration received by SLED before the security officer begins duties at a client site. The required written examination must be designed by the company certified training officer and must consist of questions taken from the lesson plan performance objectives used by the trainer. Applicants who successfully complete the basic training will, upon issuance of a registration card by SLED, be designated as a Registered Private Security Officer.

An alternative basic training course approved by SLED may be substituted for standard basic training. For consideration of approval by

SLED, an alternative training course must be developed and conducted by an agency or educational institution accredited by a nationally recognized accreditation authority recognized by SLED. Any applicant who successfully completes alternative basic training will, upon employment by a licensed private security entity, qualify for registration by SLED as a Certified Private Security Officer.

Additionally, a security officer applicant must complete an additional minimum two hours of orientation and training by a certified company training officer. The training must be sufficient to ensure:

- the safe, accurate and proper use of equipment to be used by the security officer;

- knowledge adequate to properly and competently perform the duties and responsibilities specific to the assignment of the officer; and,

- additional topics specified by the employer.

If you want to be licensed to carry a firearm while on duty as a security officer, there is an added training requirement. In addition to the training discussed above, a private security officer who will be authorized to carry a firearm must, before being issued, authorized or permitted to carry a firearm on duty, successfully complete a course approved by SLED, consisting of a minimum of four hours of training by a private security company certified training officer or law enforcement firearms instructor currently certified by the South Carolina Criminal Justice Academy, in the safe and proper use of the specific type(s) of firearm(s) to be issued or carried. This firearm training must:

- adhere to the lesson plan(s) and course(s) of fire provided by the South Carolina Technical College Private Security Training School; and,

- include a demonstration of the safe and competent use of the firearm on a range supervised and documented by a private security company certified training officer or law enforcement firearms instructor currently certified by the South Carolina Criminal Justice Academy.

It is important that you keep records of all training for licensure. Accurate and complete documentation of all training of each private security officer must be retained by the employer and submitted to SLED as required. Complete and legible copies of each employee's training records must be furnished by the employer to the employee and must be retained by the employee as his permanent training record. Upon request by SLED, training documentation must be made available by the employing entity and the employee for inspection.

Upon change of employer, a registered private security officer must furnish to the new employer documentation of all training received. If such documentation is not available and cannot be secured from the immediate past employer, the new employer is required to conduct and document currently required minimum training. Mere possession of a registration card does not serve as documentation of required training.

Failure of an employer and registered security officer to retain required training records is a violation punishable by suspension or revocation of the company license and the security officer's registration. Private security officers must not be issued or use equipment or devices for which they have not successfully completed training adequate to ensure the proper, accurate and safe use of such equipment.

Documentation of such training must be maintained by the licensee and be available for inspection by SLED.

The permit application and renewal must specifically reauthorize the type of firearm to be used by the applicant while acting as a security officer. This means that the security officer must choose the firearm to be used for security officer work. The applicant must thereafter prove proficiency with that specific firearm and only become licensed to use that particular firearm while on duty as a security officer. This firearm must also be approved or issued by the security officer's employer.

Once issued the license, a person issued a Security Weapons Permit may only carry a firearm in an open and fully-exposed manner while in uniform and performing security duties or while in a vehicle enroute directly to or from a security post or place of assignment. If the security operation requires the security officer to carry a concealed weapon, each security officer must obtain a Security Concealed Weapons Permit.

Security *Concealed* Weapons Permit

In its discretion, SLED may issue a Security Concealed Weapons Permit to a registered security officer to carry, whether concealed or not, a firearm about his person, even though he is not in uniform or on duty if SLED determines that the additional permit would enable the security officer to better perform his assigned duties. The authority conveyed by the permit may be restricted by SLED. A violation of any rules associated with a Security Weapons Permit or a Security Concealed Weapons Permit is a misdemeanor and can also bring civil penalties. Further, if you commit another crime while on duty like aggravated assault or manslaughter, you will face felony charges.

Remember that a Security Concealed Weapons Permit under Section 40-18-100 is completely different from a Concealed Weapons

Permit under Section 23-31-205 et seq., South Carolina Code of Laws. While these licenses seem very similar, the Security Concealed Weapons Permit is less defined and leaves the holder more open to confusion than a Concealed Weapons Permit. SLED makes a determination for each individual applicant and tailors the Security Concealed Weapons Permit to that applicant. Therefore, one permit holder may have a completely different set of rules than another permit holder.

Even though it seems that a Security Concealed Weapons Permit grants the holder the same authority as a Concealed Weapons Permit, it remains advisable for Security Concealed Weapons Permit holders to also get a Concealed Weapons Permit. Getting both is probably redundant but it prevents any gaps or ambiguities between the two permits.

Summary Points

- Gun ranges enjoy special protections under South Carolina law.

- The so-called "assault weapons" ban is no longer law.

- Most active and retired law enforcement officers can carry concealed weapons nationwide in accordance with the Law Enforcement Officers Safety Act.

- South Carolina Law provides for a security officer weapons permit and a security officers concealed weapons permits that are distinct from the general Concealed Weapons Permit (CWP).

Chapter 9
Conclusion

Your Brain is your First Line of Defense

In South Carolina and the United States, you have gun rights that are the envy of much of the world. A firearm gives you a powerful weapon to repel criminals, drug-crazed maniacs, terrorists, foreign governments and even possible tyranny from our own government.

Remember, however, that your brain is your first line of defense. Think about dangerous places and situations and avoid them. Think about ways to secure your home and property so that criminals pass you by for easier targets. Take firearms and self-defense training courses together with family and friends. Support politicians and organizations that take strong stances supporting your right to keep and bear arms. If you do not have one already, get your concealed weapons permit and carry your gun with you. Finally, read this book again and feel free to contact us with any questions that you have.

South Carolina and the United States need more people who are willing to own and legally carry firearms for legitimate self-defense. However, if you do choose to possess and carry firearms, strive to be an intelligent and responsible gun owner. Look first for ways to protect your family, yourself and your property with your brains instead of bullets.

What You should have Learned from this Book

This book has given you a good look at South Carolina weapons law. You should now be more competent to possess, carry and assess the appropriateness of using a weapon. You should also have gotten the message to get a concealed weapons permit if you do not already have one.

The Bottom Line

Self-defense is a fundamental human right. But defending yourself can be dangerous if you don't have the tools. The tools that you need are your weapons and knowledge of the law. We hope that this book has helped you understand the law. If it has not, read it again. If it has, tell a friend to get a copy.

Appendix I
Federal Firearms Disability and Removing a Legal Disability

Federal Firearms Disability in General

Under federal law, there are nine categories of persons prohibited from possessing firearms. It is a federal felony for you to possess a firearm if you are a:

- Person under indictment for, or convicted of, any crime punishable by imprisonment for a term exceeding one year (most violent felonies and some misdemeanors);

- Fugitive from justice;

- Person who is an unlawful user of, or addicted to, any controlled substance;

- Person who has been declared by a court as mental defectives or has been committed to a mental institution;

- Illegal alien, or alien who was admitted to the United States under a nonimmigrant visa;

- Person who has been dishonorably discharged from the Armed Forces;

- Person who has renounced his or her United States citizenship;

- Person subject to certain types of restraining orders; or

- Person who has been convicted of a misdemeanor crime of domestic violence.

People who are prevented from possessing firearms under federal law are commonly said to have a *lifetime federal firearms disability.*

How do you know if you have a legal disability?

First, those with a Federal or State felony conviction almost always have a legal disability. More specifically, according to 18 United States Code (U.S.C.) 922(g), you have a legal disability if one of the following applies to you:

- **Criminal** - you have been convicted in any court of a crime punishable by imprisonment for a term exceeding one year;

- **Fugitive** - you are a fugitive from justice;

- **Drugs** - you are an unlawful user of, or are addicted to any controlled substance (as defined in section 102 of the Controlled Substances Act (21 U.S.C. 802));

- **Insanity** - you have been adjudicated as a mental defective or you have been committed to a mental institution;

- **Aliens** - you are an alien and are illegally or unlawfully in the United States; or have been admitted to the United States under a nonimmigrant visa (as that term is defined in section 101(a)(26) of the Immigration and Nationality Act (8 U.S.C. 1101(a)(26))). This prohibition does not apply to aliens who are law enforcement officers of a friendly nation and are on law enforcement business, are designated by the State Department as a foreign official or a distinguished foreign visitor, are admitted to the USA for hunting or sporting purposes or have a lawful hunting license, or are an official representative of a foreign government under certain conditions as provided in 18 USC 922(y)(2);

- **Court Martial** - you have been discharged from the Armed Forces under dishonorable conditions;

- **Renunciation of Citizenship** - you have renounced your United States citizenship;

- **Violence Injunctions** - you are subject to a court order that was issued after a hearing of which you received actual notice, and at which you had an opportunity to participate; restrains you from harassing, stalking, or threatening your intimate partner or your child or the child of your intimate partner, or engaging in other conduct that would place your intimate partner in reasonable fear of bodily injury to such partner or child; and (C)(i) the order includes a finding that you represent a credible threat to the physical safety of your intimate partner or your child or the child of your intimate partner; or (ii) the order by its terms explicitly prohibits the use, attempted use, or threatened use of physical force against your intimate partner or child that would reasonably be expected to cause bodily injury; or

- **Domestic Violence Conviction** - you have been convicted in any court of a misdemeanor crime of domestic violence.

What is a crime punishable by a term of imprisonment exceeding one year?

Those who have been convicted of a crime with a potential jail term of more than 1 year are burdened with a federal firearms disability. This disability is based on the maximum potential penalty that you could have been given for the crime. It is not based on the sentence the convict actually receives. If the convict received a sentence of two years probation, but could have gone to jail for up to 5 years, the legal disability applies because of the potential term of 5 years.

However, there are a couple of exceptions to the above general rule. 18 U.S.C. 921((a)20) specifically says that any Federal or State offense pertaining to antitrust violations, unfair trade practices, restraints of trade, or other similar offenses relating to the regulation of business practices is exempted from this definition. Therefore if you are convicted of a crime and could have gone to jail for more than 1 year but the crime involved an antitrust violation; you do not have a legal disability.

The same statute also provides an exception for *state* crimes which are misdemeanors in the state of conviction and which carry a maximum term of imprisonment of 2 years of less. This one is pretzel logic, we know. The general rule is that a legal disability arises when a person is convicted for crimes punishable by imprisonment of more than 1 year. Then the statute excludes state misdemeanors which are punishable by imprisonment for 2 years or less. This contradiction is prima facia evidence that the federal government's right hand does not know what its' left hand is doing. Anyway, this means that if you were convicted of a state misdemeanor that is punishable by up to two years in prison, you do not have a legal disability.

If I plead guilty to a felony, does that mean I was convicted?

Under 18 USC 921(a)(20), the definition of a conviction is based on the law of the jurisdiction where the proceedings were held. If the proceedings were in South Carolina, you will be out of luck. Section 16-23-10(6) of the South Carolina Code of Laws defines a conviction as all cases which end in pleas of guilty, pleas of nolo conterndere, or forfeiture of bond. This statute directly defines the term for purposes of handgun crimes (South Carolina Code of Laws Section 16-23 et seq.).

The bottom line is that, if you plead guilty, nolo conterndere, or had a forfeiture of a bond in a South Carolina court to a crime that is a felony that carries a potential penalty of greater than 1 year in jail (or misdemeanor that carries a potential penalty of more than 2 years in jail), you have a legal disability. If the proceedings were held in another jurisdiction and you plead to the charges, you may or may not have a legal disability depending upon that state's definition of conviction.

What if I was convicted of a felony but didn't have an attorney?

Sorry you are out of luck. Unfortunately, if you didn't get an attorney; the federal law does not relieve you of your legal disability. If you are charged with a crime, you should always seriously consider hiring an attorney. We're not trying to generate business here, it is just a simple fact that your chances of a favorable outcome increase dramatically if you are represented by competent counsel.

What if my Felony has been pardoned or expunged?

18 U.S.C. 921(a)(20) provides that any conviction which has been expunged, or set aside, or for which a person has been pardoned or has had civil rights restored shall **not** be considered a conviction for purposes of this chapter, **unless** such pardon, expungement, or restoration of civil rights expressly provides that the person may not ship, transport, possess, or receive firearms. This means that if you have a conviction for a crime which would normally make you ineligible, but you have been pardoned or achieved an expungement; you generally do not have a legal disability. It is important that any conditions or terms of the pardon or expungement do not provide specific language that prohibits you from shipping, transporting, possessing or receiving firearms. So, if you have already received a pardon or expungement, and the authorities placed a condition or term in your pardon or expungement that prohibits you from shipping, transporting, possessing, or receiving firearms; you still have a legal disability. If your pardon or expungement has no such specific prohibition, your legal disability has been removed. If you are seeking a pardon or expungement, it is wise to make every effort to ensure that your pardon or expungement will not

have any specific firearms terms or conditions. Without a specific firearm term or condition, the pardon or expungement will remove your legal disability.

What if I plead nolo contendre to a crime of domestic violence?

Again, 18 USC 921(a)(20) bases the definition of a conviction on the law of the jurisdiction where the proceedings were held. If the proceedings were in the State of South Carolina, you will be out of luck. The South Carolina Code of Laws define *conviction* as cases that end in pleas of guilty, pleas of nolo conterndere, or forfeiture of bond (Section 16-23-10(6)). Therefore, if you plead nolo conterndere in a South Carolina court to domestic violence, you have a legal disability. If the proceedings were held in another jurisdiction and you plead to the charges, you may not have a legal disability. In that case, you must determine that state's definition of *conviction*.

What if I was convicted of a crime of domestic violence but didn't have an attorney?

There may be good news for you, 18 USC 921(a)(33)(B)(i) provides that a person shall not be considered to have been convicted of a crime of domestic violence, unless the person was represented by counsel in the case, or knowingly and intelligently waived the right to counsel in the case; *and* in the case of a prosecution for such an offense for which the person was entitled to a jury trial in the jurisdiction in which the case was tried, the person must have either been tried by a jury, or the person must have knowingly and intelligently waived the right to have the case tried by a jury, by guilty plea or otherwise.

If you didn't have any attorney, you might not have too much room for excitement because, in most cases, you will probably be found to have knowingly and intelligently waived that right. If you did not waive that right, the court almost certainly appointed you an attorney.

The same is true of trial by jury. If you were entitled to one, the court almost always makes sure you either get one or knowingly and intelligently waive that right. If you knowingly and intelligently waived either of these rights, you still have the legal disability. So, even if you did not have an attorney or did not have a trial by jury, you probably still have the disability. However, if you have real doubts about whether you legitimately waived your right to an attorney and trial, you might want to speak with a lawyer and make the argument.

What if my crime of domestic violence has been pardoned or expunged?

If your federal firearms disability is the result of domestic violence (even if it was a state misdemeanor charge with a potential penalty of greater than 2 years in jail), Section 18 USC 921(a)(33)(B)(ii) provides for identical results as for felonies under 18 U.S.C. 921(a)(20). So, look at the section above that deals with expungement or pardons of felonies for guidance.

Removal of a Legal Disability

The South Carolina Constitution gives the executive branch the power to grant full or conditional pardons and to restore the civil rights of criminals convicted under state of South Carolina crimes. This power is also referred to as executive clemency. It is totally within the discretion of the executive branch. This means that if you are denied, you cannot file a lawsuit to have a court review the denial. It also means that writing to your state representative or state senator won't do you any good. The South Carolina Executive Branch has no authority to pardon federal crimes.

Removal of a legal disability for federal crimes was settled in the court case _Beecham v. United States_. In that case, the U.S. Supreme Court held that those convicted under most federal felonies (or misdemeanors with a potential jail term of over 1 year) remain subject to the federal firearms disability until their civil rights are restored through a federal, not a state, procedure. Therefore, those convicted of violating certain federal crimes (who have had their civil rights restored by a state law or procedure) are still, nonetheless, prohibited by federal law from possessing firearms.

Unfortunately for those convicted under a federal crime, there is no general federal statutory procedure for restoring civil rights to federal felons. While the Bureau of Alcohol, Tobacco and Firearms (BATF) is authorized under 18 U.S.C. 925(c) to restore federal firearms privileges to an individual convicted of a felony, it has not been permitted to expend funds for this purpose since fiscal year 1992 (although it may restore rights to corporations). So, at this time, an individual that has been burdened with a federal firearms disability may extinguish the disability only through a presidential pardon.

Eligibility

Eligibility for a pardon is based upon the type of sentence you initially received. If you:

- received probation, you must be discharged from supervision, pay all restitution, and pay all other fees associated with the criminal conviction;

- were sentenced to go to jail and were released on parole, you must pay all restitution and other fees. You must also either complete five years of parole or if your maximum parole period is less than five years, you must complete the maximum;

- were sentenced to jail and have served all of your time, you are eligible when you pay all restitution and all other fees associated with the criminal charge;

- are still in jail, you must have extraordinary circumstances which warrant the granting of the pardon. You must also pay all restitution and all other fees associated with the criminal charge; finally,

- are still in jail but have an illness, if the illness is terminal and you have a life expectancy of one year or less, you can apply as long as you have paid all restitution and all other fees.

How do I apply for Executive Clemency?

Your application for executive clemency begins by getting an application from the South Carolina Department of Probation. You then carefully fill-out the application and send the completed application, along with letters of reference and a fee of $100 to the Department of Probation.

Application

The application itself is a simple two page form. It asks for general information like your name, address, and social security number. It also asks more invasive questions like all prior arrests and convictions. You then have to dig through your memory or records for every address and place of employment for the past five (5) years. Finally, you must give the reason **why** you are seeking the pardon. The reason might be that you want to go out and get a gun or that you want a gun around the house. In the application however, you might want to present that reason a little more subtly.

Certified Copies of Documents

Once you have the application completely filled out, you will need to attach certified copies of all documents showing that all the restitution and other fees associated with the criminal charge have been paid in full. Certified copies are not simple photocopies. Certified copies are photocopies that are made by the Clerk of Court or other authorized official. The copies must be made directly from the original court file or the official records by the clerk. Further, a certified copy will include a certification, by the clerk, placed upon the photocopy. A certification is a stamp, crimp, seal or other mark placed upon the photocopy that includes language to the effect that the clerk certifies that the photocopy is a true and accurate reproduction of the official original.

Fees for Certified Documents

Almost always, the clerk charges a fee for the certified copies. Be prepared to pay the fee in cash or money order because many times the clerk will not accept a personal check or credit card. Word to the wise, any time you need certified copies, call the clerk for the exact amount of the fee and stop at the ATM to get the appropriate amount of cash before going to the courthouse. If you are using the mail, mail only money orders and not personal checks. If you don't send a money order or cashier's check, the clerk will invariably send you back your paperwork and you'll be back to square one.

Courthouse Security

One more word to the wise, if you go into the courthouse, you will usually have to go through a security check with metal detectors. You can make this check much easier by bringing minimal "stuff" with you into the courthouse. Leave your chrome motorcycle keychain, pocketknife, and historic pewter dip cans in the car. If you are going into a federal courthouse, leave your cell phone, pager, blackberry, and PDA in the car too because they will not let you bring them in.

Letters of Reference

You will need to include three letters of reference along with your application. As a practical matter, look for people who know you well and who are in a position to observe your current behavior and character.

The letters should include the name, address, home phone number, and work phone number of each person who is writing the letter of reference. The letters must be recently dated and must be signed by the person vouching for your character.

Application Fee

When you mail off your application, you must include the application fee. Currently, the fee is $100 and it must be paid by money order or cashier's check. It should be made out to: The South Carolina Department of Probation, Parole, and Pardon Services. Like your request for certified copies, if you fail to include the fee in the proper form, they will return the application to you unprocessed and you'll be back to square one.

The Role of the Department

Once you have sent off a complete and accurate application, your fate is in the hands of the Department of Probation, Parole, and Pardon Services. They will verify all the information contained in your application, including the references. The Department generally requires about seven to nine months from the time you file the application until the date of your pardon hearing.

A pardon hearing is where you will orally present your reasons why you should be pardoned to a single or multiple decision-makers. You will be notified where and when the hearing is being held. The proceeding will have courtroom type decorum so you should conduct yourself as if you were about to go to court. You should be dressed in a suit and tie if you are male or business attire if you are female. Speak only after first standing up and use your best manners towards the decision makers and all others at the hearing. The hearing should last less than an hour.

It is preferable that you have a lawyer for this hearing but it is not required. If possible, you should elicit witnesses and testimony favorable to you and include evidence that will help you. If you do not have a lawyer, follow the instructions that the Board provides you with regarding allowable witnesses and evidence.

If you are denied a pardon, the decision of the Board is final for that application. Because this is not a judicial proceeding, there is no appeal and there is nothing you can do except reapply. There is nothing that prevents you from reapplying immediately. However, as a practical matter, you should probably give yourself a little time to further improve your circumstances. Alternatively, if the membership of the board changes you can reapply and hope for better results with the new board.

Appendix II
Getting the Qualified Non-Resident Form R-168

If you are a qualified non-resident, your completed SLED Form R-168 must be signed by the county assessor in which your South Carolina property is located. It might be a good idea here to review dealing with government offices, certified copies and certification of documents. We discussed certified copies earlier in Appendix I but you might not have had a need to read that Appendix.

If you need an official document from a government official, you should always have a game plan before getting into your car and driving to the government office. If you don't, there is a great chance that you will waste a lot of time and get very frustrated. You might waste time driving through downtown streets looking for the office. You might waste time wandering around the building looking for your office. And worst of all, you might waste time standing in the wrong line.

The three best planning tools are this book, the internet and your phone. After reading this book, search the internet or your phone book for phone numbers and addresses. Make sure that you call the office first and find out who you need to see to get what you want. Find out which office they are in and verify the address. Sometimes the official will give you directions or landmarks. If they are not too busy, they often help with other valuable advice like where to park and when the office goes out for lunch. Mainly though, try to identify a specific person in the office who is familiar with issuing the type of document that you are looking for. A Plan, don't leave home without it.

As an example, we investigated getting a SLED Form R-168 from the Greenville County Assessor's Office. The first number that appeared on the County's website connected us to an automated phone router that started with the, "press one for this, press two for that" routine. After pushing quite a few buttons and getting forwarded to several live employees, we were directed to the precise office that we needed. Then, within that office the staff had to ask around for the person in the office with experience with the SLED Form R-168. After a few more seconds on hold and more forwarding to different desks, we were finally speaking to the precise person who actually issues the Form R-168 certification.

This is not at all meant to be a criticism of the Greenville County office. The office was very courteous, concerned and helpful. It is probably just relatively rare that the staff gets a call from an out-of-state property owner looking for a SLED Form R-168. Once we found the right person, she knew exactly what to do. The point here is to spend the time in the comfort of your home reading the internet and calling the government offices instead of driving around downtown streets and wandering around buildings.

Another important point is that certified copies are not regular photocopies. You will not need a certified copy of the SLED Form R-168. Instead, the official will issue the original that you have brought to the official's desk. But, if SLED requires supplemental information from you beyond your original application, they might ask for certified copies of some documents.

Certified copies are photocopies that are made by the Clerk of Court or other authorized official. The copies must be made directly from the original court file or the official records by the clerk. Further, a certified copy will include a certification, by the clerk, placed upon the photocopy. A certification is a stamp, crimp, seal or other mark placed upon the photocopy that includes language to the effect that the clerk certifies that the photocopy is a true and accurate reproduction of the official original.

Almost always, the clerk charges a fee for certified copies. Be prepared to pay the fee in cash or money order because many times the clerk will not accept a personal check or credit card. Word to the wise,

235

any time you need certified copies, call the clerk for the exact amount of the fee and stop at the ATM to get the appropriate amount of cash before going to the courthouse. If you are using the mail, send only money orders or cashier's checks and not send personal checks. If you don't send a money order or cashier's check, the clerk will invariably send back your paperwork and you'll be back to square one.

Courthouse Security

One more word to the wise, if you go into the courthouse, you will usually have to go through a security check with metal detectors. Many larger counties have public records offices separate from the courthouse but the smaller counties often have "all-in-one" buildings.

You can make this check much easier by bringing minimal "stuff" with you into the courthouse. Leave your chrome motorcycle key chains, pocketknives, and your prized historic pewter dip cans in the car. If you are going into a federal courthouse, leave your cell phone, pager, blackberry, or PDA in the car too because they won't let you bring one in. Federal marshals will not even let you store the electronic device with them or in or near the building. Instead, you will end up walking back to your car to store your device.

Appendix III
Fingerprints

This Appendix describes the process of obtaining fingerprints in greater detail than the body of the book. First, you should call a qualified law enforcement agency convenient to you and ask for the hours of public fingerprinting. (For brevity's sake, I will substitute "qualified law enforcement agency" or SLED approved fingerprint technician with simply "police station.") Sometimes, you can pop in to a police station and get an officer to provide fingerprints. However, this is the exception rather than the rule. You are well advised to call the police department's non-emergency number and ask for a firm confirmation of their fingerprinting hours.

Remember that any police station can complete your fingerprint card. If you live closer to a North Carolina police station than a South Carolina one, feel free to get your prints at the North Carolina station (they might be able to charge you more though). If you are a student, you might be able to go to your university police station. If you are a qualified non-resident and live in Washington, D.C., feel free to go the J. Edgar Hoover Building and get fingerprinted by the FBI there. The point is that you can get your prints done at any police or law enforcement station. Before wasting your time and gas, though, make sure that you are driving to a bona-fide police office that will do fingerprints for you.

Once you have confirmed a time to arrive at the police station, bring the two cards provided by SLED, your driver's license or other qualified identification and the required fee in cash or money order. You will then enter the police station and usually find a reception window. Inform the reception officer that you are there to get fingerprints. The reception officer will generally have you sit in the reception area and wait for a police officer to come through some door to greet you. You can use the time to verify that you have the fingerprint cards, a valid ID and the cash with you.

After the officer greets you, you will be led down a hall to the fingerprint area. The office will have either an old fashioned wood and steel fingerprint board or a new-fangled digital imager. The main difference is that the old type requires that your fingers roll in a washable ink and the new type does not require ink. Both require that the officer take your hand and roll your fingers, thumbs and palms over the imaging surface.

Try to keep your hands and fingers very loose and allow the officer to do all of the work. There is a tendency to try to roll your fingers yourself but that might cause you to blur the image. If you are getting a digital image the officer can cancel the image before printing it on the card but if you are using the ink, a blur can require you to get a new card and come back another day. Try to relax and let the officer do all of the work.

Your fingerprint cards will have spaces for information. Be sure to fill out all of the information requested. Be very careful to have the officer place his or her information on the card also. Again, I say, be careful to get this information from the officer because even the most innocent person has a primeval urge to get out of a police station as fast as possible. If you do not get the information and signature of the officer, your application will be rejected.

About the Authors

Dr. Steve Shaw is a practicing attorney in both South Carolina and Florida. He holds a J.D. and a Ph.D. from the University of Florida and was the recipient of the Computer Assisted Legal Instruction (CALI) book award in legal history. He served for several years on staff with U.S. Representative Cliff Stearns who has led the charge for a national right to carry law since 1995. His interests include firearms and tactical training, writing and legal education. He holds a defensive pistol certificate from the Defensive Training Group and a CWP in both South Carolina and Florida. His memberships include the NRA and the Ocala Sportsmen's Association. He is very happily married to his South Carolina native wife Melanie Donna.

Jim Kelley graduated from the University of Florida College of Law and has been a litigation attorney for over 10 years. With a lifelong interest in weapons, he has developed a deep knowledge of firearms law. He is a member of the International Defensive Pistol Association and the NRA and his training includes target and combat shooting as well as hand-to-hand defensive tactics. Jim holds a Florida CWP.

G. Curtis Moore, Jr. is lifelong South Carolina resident with over 21 years of law enforcement experience. His Military Police experience includes action in both Operation Just Cause in Panama and Operation Desert Storm in the Middle East. He holds a degree in Criminal Justice from Piedmont Technical College. He was a City of Greenwood police officer for seven years and is now a sergeant at Lander University.

About the Legislative Consultant

Dr. Robert D. Butler has an interesting blend of educational achievements. He started with a B.S. in Social Science Multi-disciplinary Studies (Political Science, Psychology, Sociology) from Michigan State University, and then he completed one half of the MBA program at Michigan State University before deciding to pursue a non business career choice. Dr. Butler next obtained a Doctor of Chiropractic degree from Sherman College of Straight Chiropractic (where he was valedictorian of his class), and then opened a private practice in Lexington, SC. After a career ending injury, Dr. Butler obtained a J.D. from the University of South Carolina School of Law where he was inducted into the Whig and Robe Society. As a handicapped person unable to physically endure working eight hours a day, Dr. Butler has instead served as a home bound volunteer legislative consultant in the fight to protect our Second Amendment rights. His training in the social sciences allowing him to better understand people, combined with his attention to detail honed as a physician, and his specialized knowledge of the law make for one unique Second Amendment activist.

Authors' Final Notes

The authors are deeply indebted to Dr. Robert Butler for his vital input and careful review of the statutes and case law discussed in this book. South Carolina gun owners also owe him a debt of gratitude for his tireless work defending the right to keep and bear arms.

The authors also wish to thank Allen Arms of Greenville, South Carolina for providing photographer Justin Berrios with the backdrop for many of the pictures in this book. We also thank the volunteer models for their participation. Last, but not least, we thank our purchasers who are establishing this book as the premier gun law resource for South Carolina.